2015 VICTORY HALL YEARBOOK

VICTORY HALL PRESS

YEARBOOK PRODUCTION:

Concept: Anne Trauben
Editors: James Pustorino, Anne Trauben
Cover Design: James Pustorino
Interior Design/Layout: Alejandro Rubin
Marketing: Danielle Brooks

VICTORY HALL PRESS
180 Grand St.
Jersey City, NJ 07302
December 2015

ISBN-13: 978-0692594469
ISBN-10: 0692594469

This program is made possible in part by funds from the New Jersey State Council on the Arts/Department of State, a partner agency of the National Endowment for the Arts, administered by the Hudson County Office of Cultural and Heritage. Affairs, Thomas A. DeGise, County Executive, and the Board of Chosen Freeholders.

TABLE OF CONTENTS

VICTORY HALL YEARBOOK 2015

We have had a busy and productive year at Victory Hall Inc. This yearbook looks at the exhibitions and programs we have produced throughout 2015 and marks the opening of our third annual BIG SMALL SHOW, a review of current painting, drawing and three dimensional works from artists in the NY/NJ metropolitan area.

BIG SMALL describes our end-of-year exhibition. We bring many small works together throughout our multiple exhibition rooms in arrangements and themes that enlarge our understanding of the elements and possibilities of art. BIG SMALL can also describe our outlook as a non-profit. We are a small organization, but we reach a lot of people.

We see a lot of possibilities, have a lot of good friends, get a lot done in a year, and hope we make a big impact. As a contemporary arts center for Jersey City, DRAWING ROOMS builds upon decades of work done in the area by visual artists in 111 First St. Studios, Pro Arts and the Jersey City Museum, as well as our own years at our Victory Hall site where we ran a community arts center from 2001-2007. This year, with three curators organizing year-round exhibitions in four locations, along with classes in two more locations, we have shown hundreds of artists and have held multiple classes and workshops each week serving many children and adults .

Victory Hall Inc. is now in our second Fellowship year of sponsor support and development training from the Geraldine R. Dodge Foundation, and has been awarded General Operating Funding grants by Hudson County through the NEA for the past decade. RAINBOW THURSDAY Artists, our weekly outreach art program for developmentally disabled adults is in its second year of CDBG funding from the city of Bayonne.

Our work with HAND-IN-HAND Art School in Bayonne was awarded a Wheat Ridge Ministries Joshua Grant this year.

The original arts center in our Victory Hall building served hundreds of children and adults each week through classes and arts programs. After a seven year absence, we are really pleased to be back in Victory Hall for our special fundraising events.

DRAWING ROOMS, now in its third year, presents professional artists from across the state of New Jersey and the New York City area regularly, and hosts visits from St Peter's Prep students, and students from Jersey City Board of Education's ATC program for those gifted in visual art, as well as OLC School student visits. These are just some of the great things that developed over 2015. There are many more detailed throughout this book. Thanks to everyone who became part of what we do this year: our funders and friends, all the artists, Fr Tom Ciba and OLC Church and School for their support, Grace Lutheran Church and Trinity Episcopal Church in Bayonne for their partnership, and our supporters at Dodge and Hudson County Cultural Affairs.

Art has an important and vital role in our communities and can add great value to our lives.
In the coming year, we look forward to working with all of you and growing together.

James Pustorino
Executive Director
Victory Hall Inc.

VICTORY HALL
DRAWING
ROOMS

Victory Hall DRAWING ROOMS is our contemporary arts center in a former convent building. With twenty rooms for individual artist or group exhibitions, gallery shop and our developing Artist Work-Spaces program, we are dedicated to providing a space where the arts communities and the public can share, interact and enjoy new artistic experiences

We produce seven or more four to eight week exhibits ranging from nine solo rooms to almost ninety in our annual Big Small Show, drawing upon a strong Jersey City artist base while reaching out across New Jersey to Brooklyn, Connecticut and Manhattan artists. Our emphasis on drawing as a basis for art creation is a core of all our curatorial direction.

It is our goal to engage the public in the process of seeing art, of talking to and working with artists, and gaining a deeper understanding their work and concepts, creating opportunities for our neighbors to own works of art and create art with the artists. We often hold multiple gatherings and receptions during the run of each exhibit to encourage as much artist/public interaction as possible. We regularly give tours and talks to schools and community groups, have an ongoing series of artist workshops, and engage in city-wide artist tour weekends. We are making a center for artists to gather, work with each other, and present their art to the public.

Launched in October 2012, we were hit hard by Hurricane Sandy and re-established our exhibition schedule in May 2013. Now in our third year, we continue to grow in all directions and we are establishing ourselves as vital institution for the visual arts in our area.

2015 marks Curator Anne Trauben's first full year of planning Drawing Rooms exhibitions. Our seven full-length exhibits plus the special Jersey City Teachers as Artists exhibit, along with our Free Artists' Workshops kept us busy all year long.

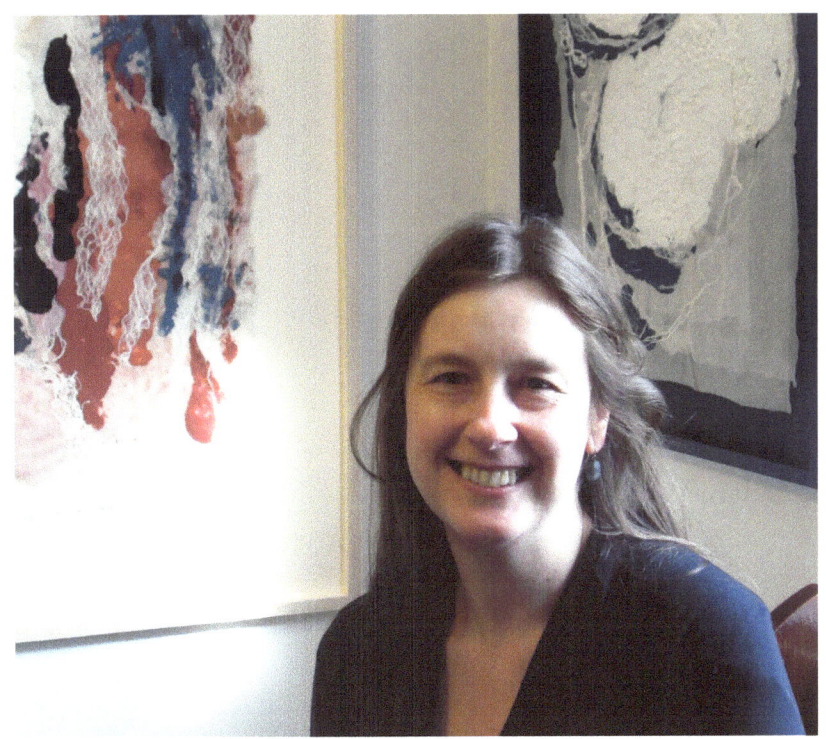
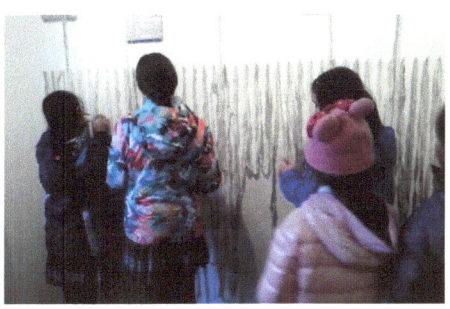
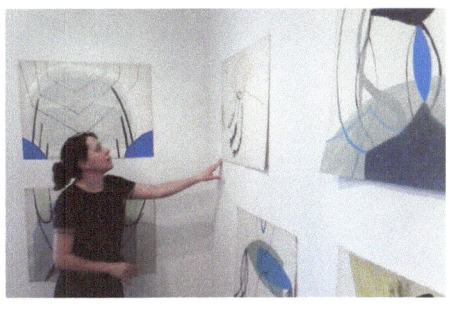
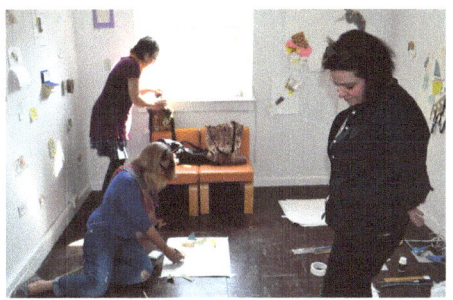
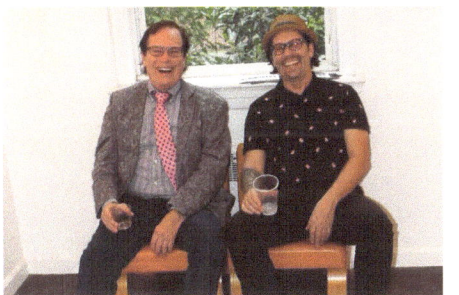
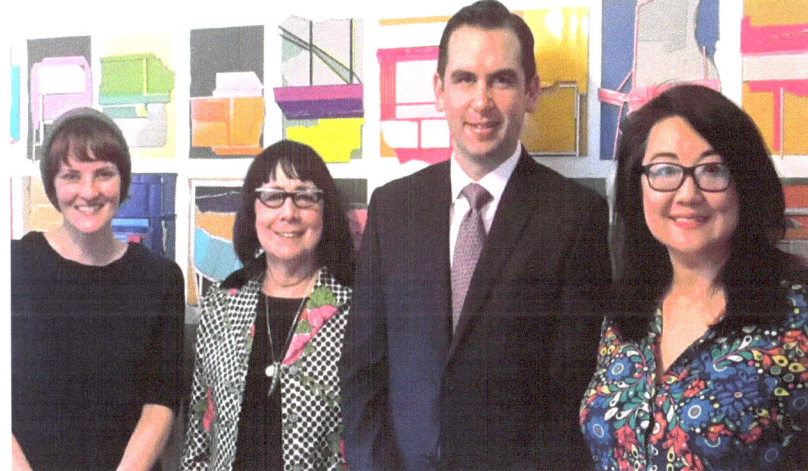
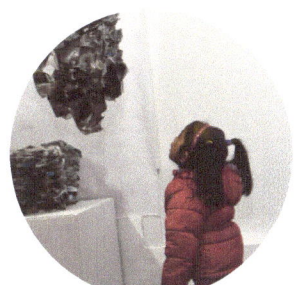
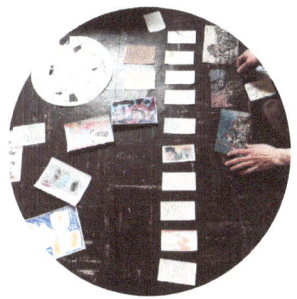
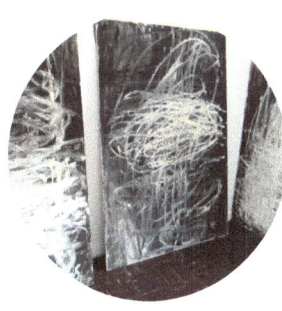
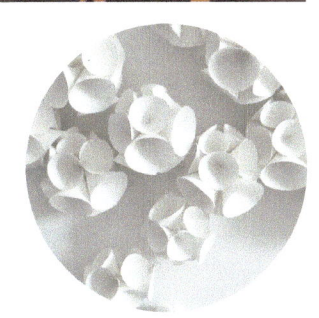
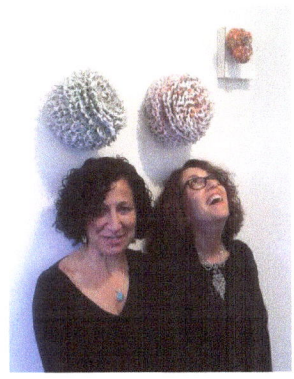
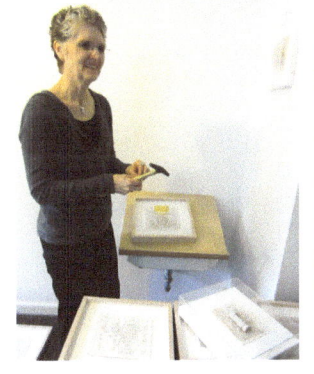
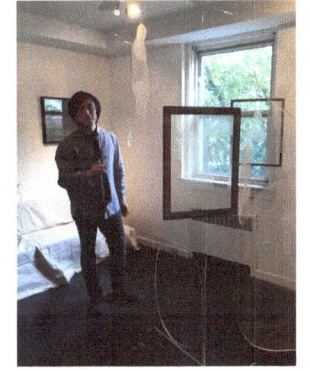
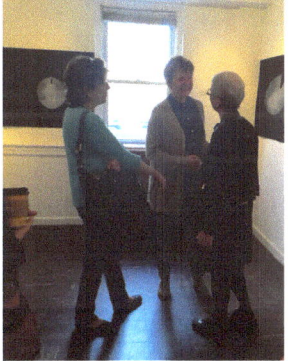

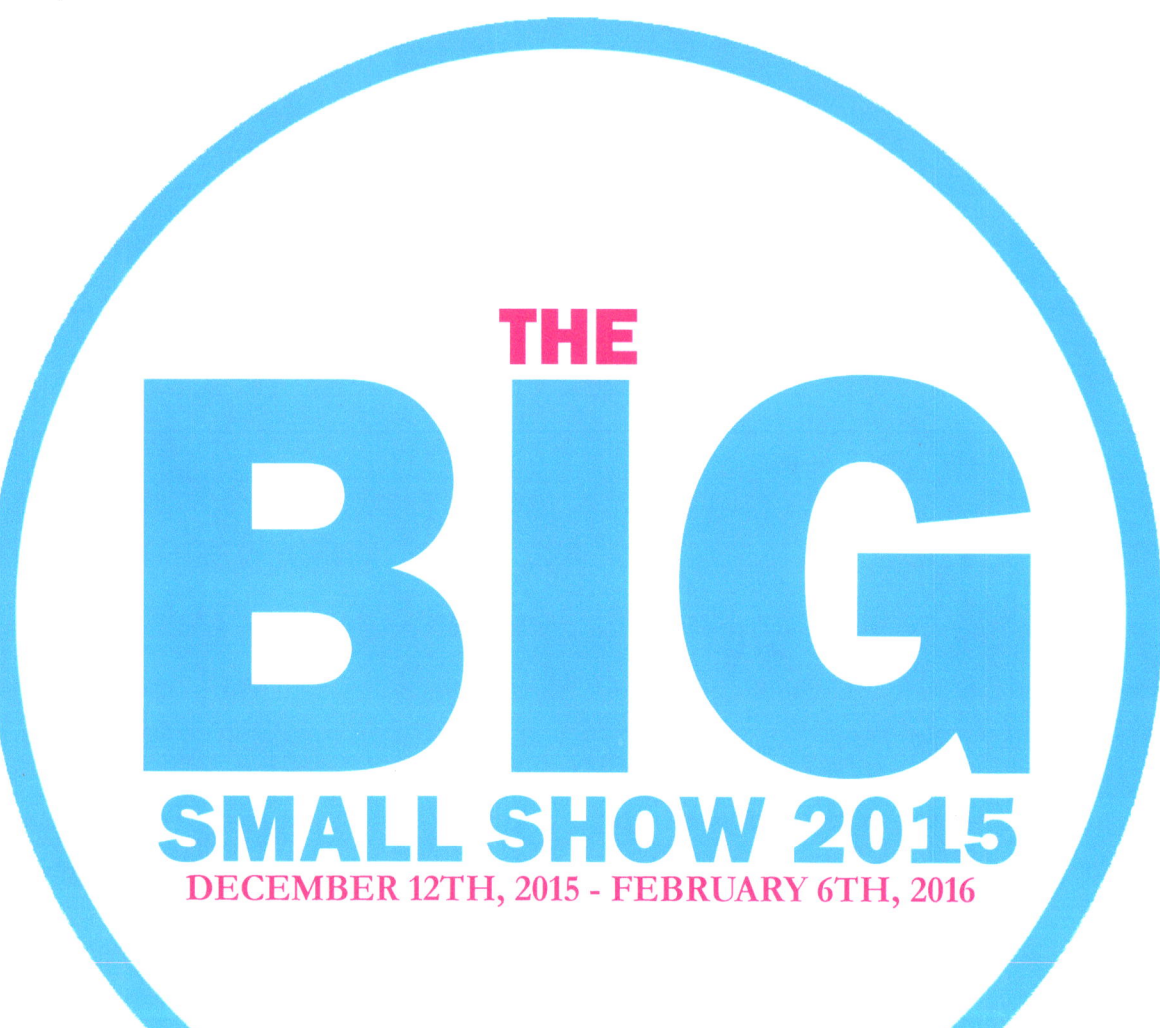

THE
BIG
SMALL SHOW 2015
DECEMBER 12TH, 2015 - FEBRUARY 6TH, 2016

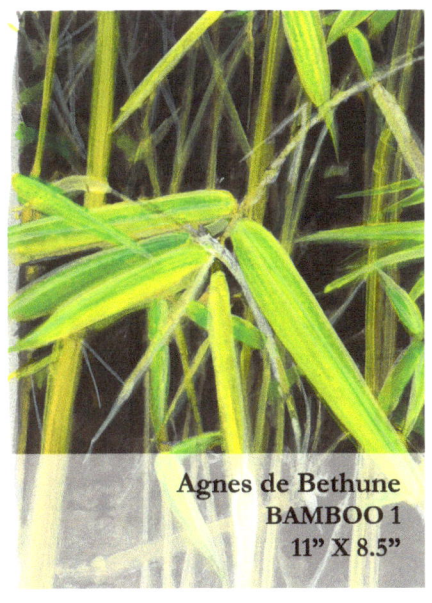

Agnes de Bethune
BAMBOO 1
11" X 8.5"

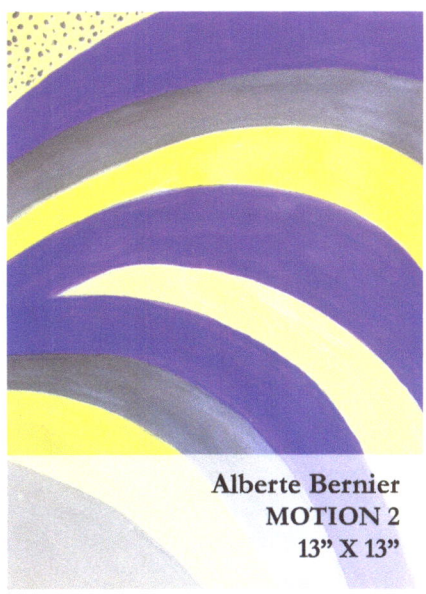

Alberte Bernier
MOTION 2
13" X 13"

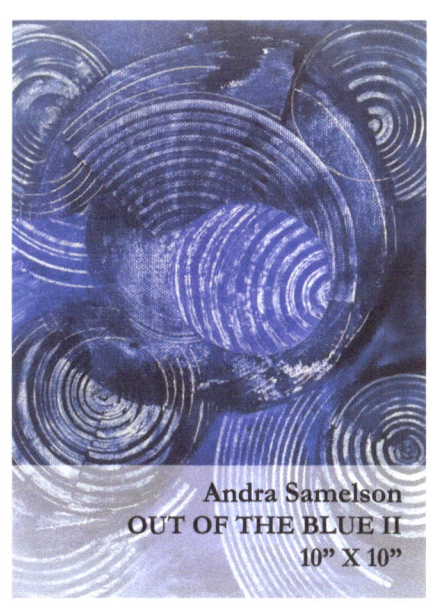

Andra Samelson
OUT OF THE BLUE II
10" X 10"

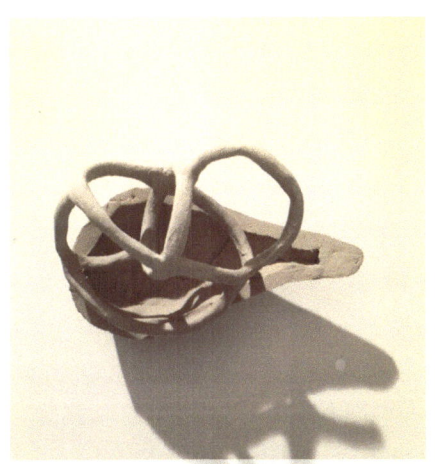

Anne Trauben
UNTITLED
2" X 3" X 5"

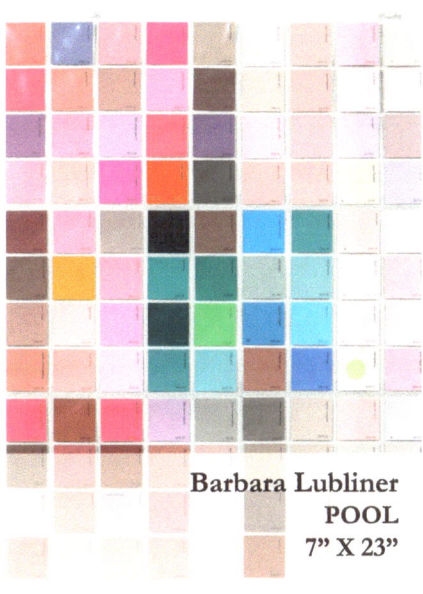

Barbara Lubliner
POOL
7" X 23"

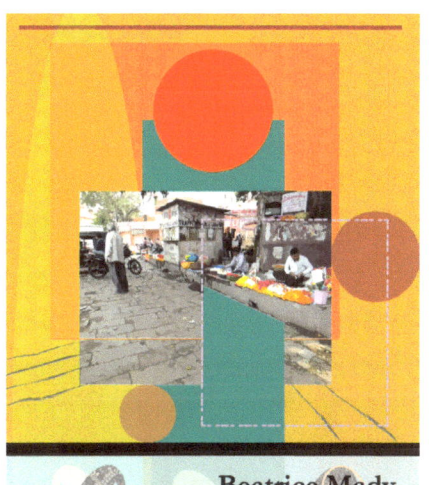

Beatrice Mady
FLOWERS FOR GARLANDS
25" X 19"

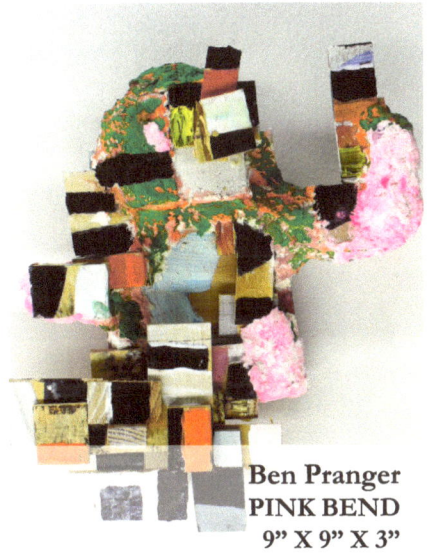

Ben Pranger
PINK BEND
9" X 9" X 3"

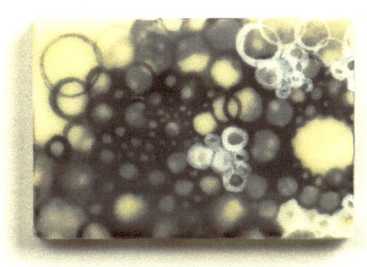

Beth Dary
TEEM 1
11" X 11"

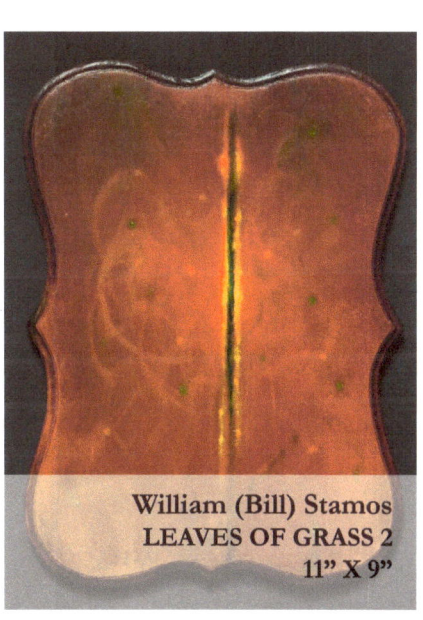

William (Bill) Stamos
LEAVES OF GRASS 2
11" X 9"

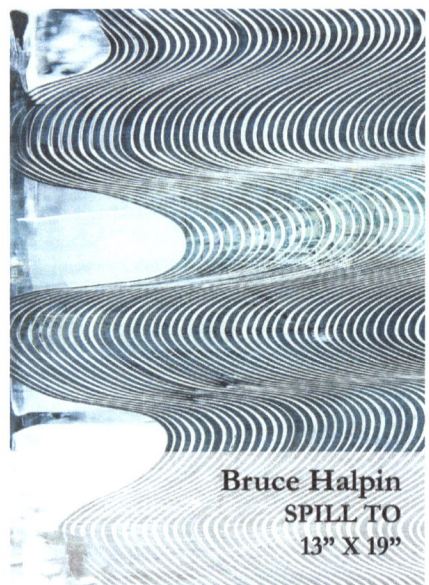

Bruce Halpin
SPILL TO
13" X 19"

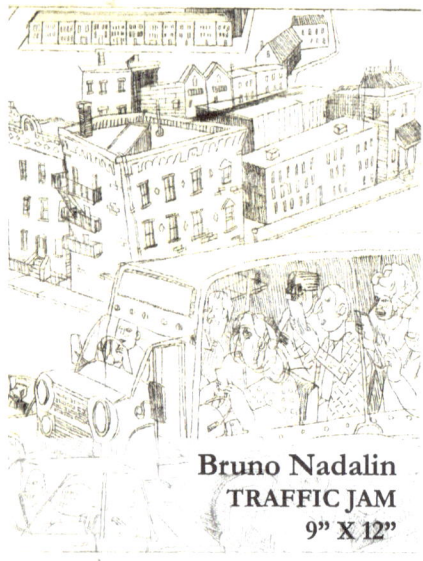

Bruno Nadalin
TRAFFIC JAM
9" X 12"

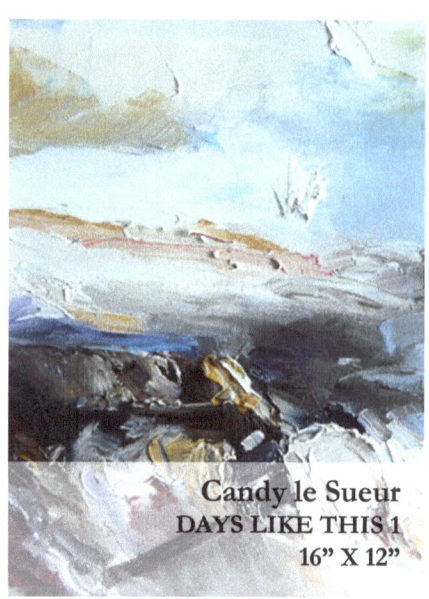

Candy le Sueur
DAYS LIKE THIS 1
16" X 12"

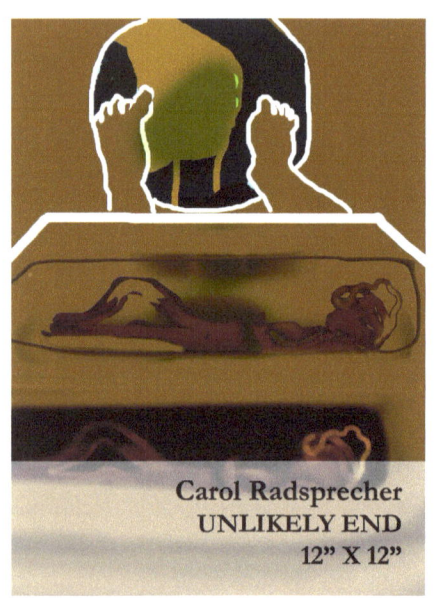

Carol Radsprecher
UNLIKELY END
12" X 12"

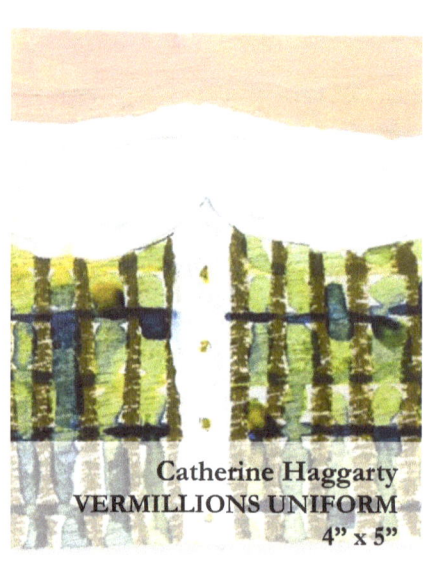

Catherine Haggarty
VERMILLIONS UNIFORM
4" x 5"

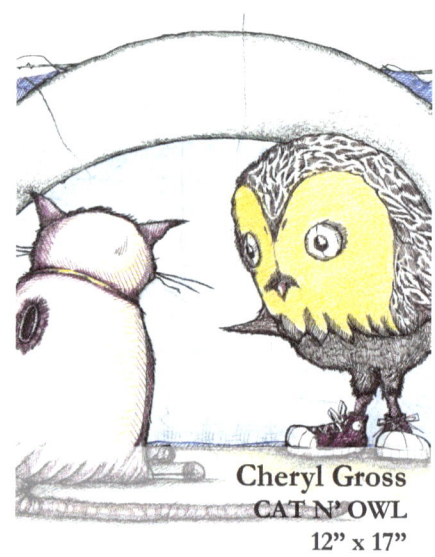

Cheryl Gross
CAT N' OWL
12" x 17"

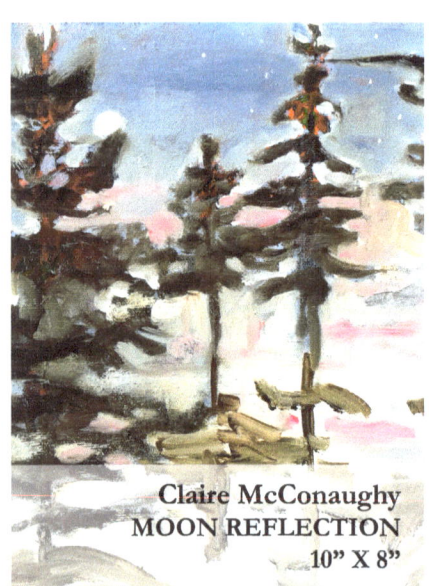

Claire McConaughy
MOON REFLECTION
10" X 8"

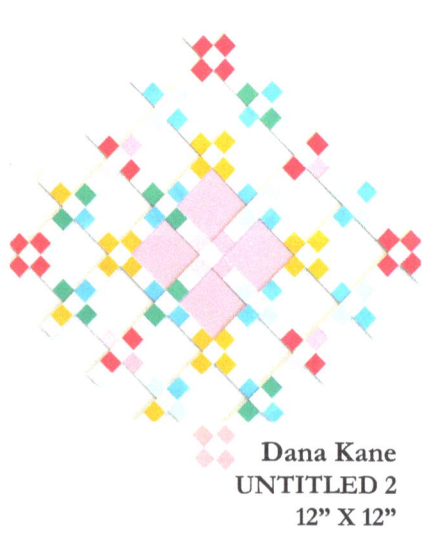

Dana Kane
UNTITLED 2
12" X 12"

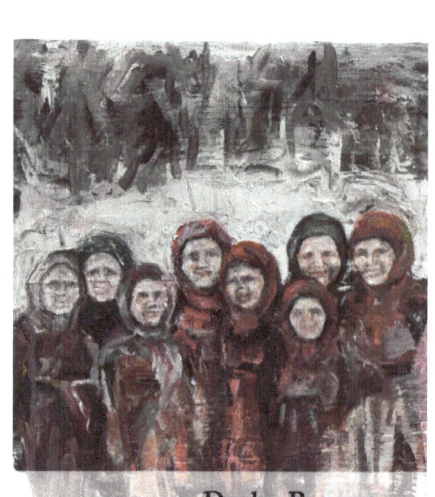

Dasha Bazanova
COUNTERPOINT GALLERY 3
H" X W"

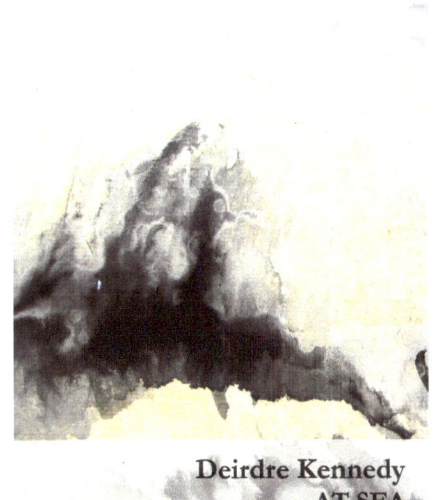

Deirdre Kennedy
AT SEA
7" X 13.5"

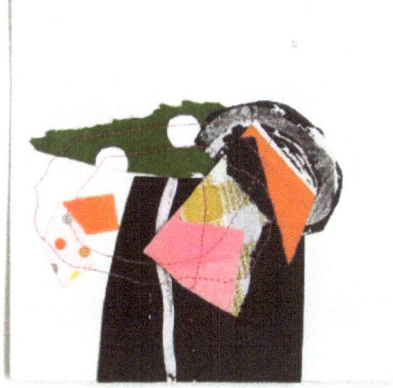

Diane Englander
PHOTO W RED AND WHITE
9.25" X 7.5"

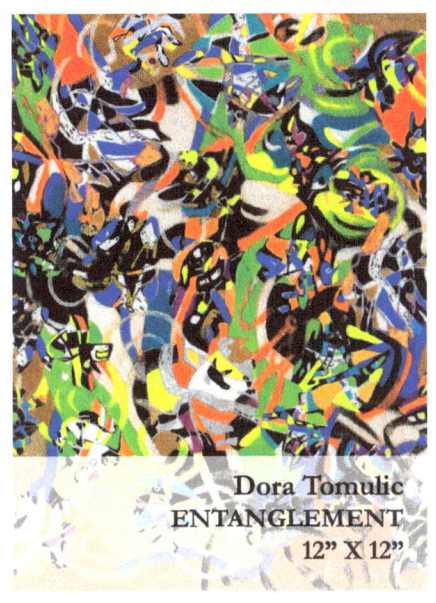

Diane June
P DOT 6
8" X 8"

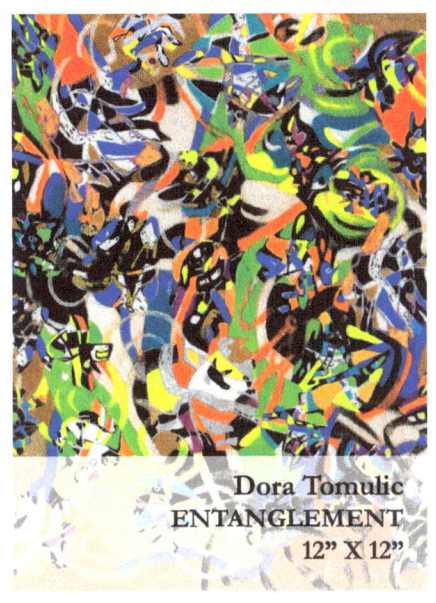

Dora Tomulic
ENTANGLEMENT
12" X 12"

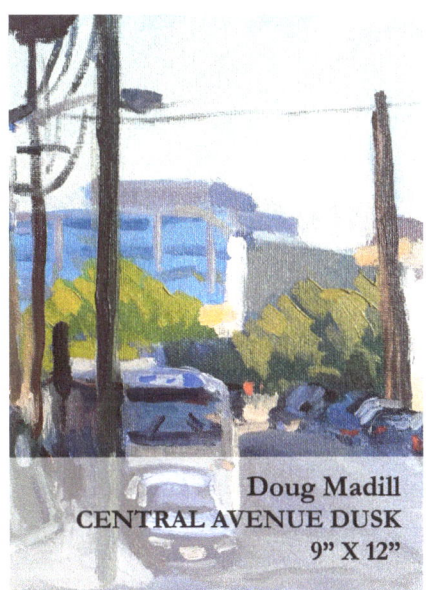

Doug Madill
CENTRAL AVENUE DUSK
9" X 12"

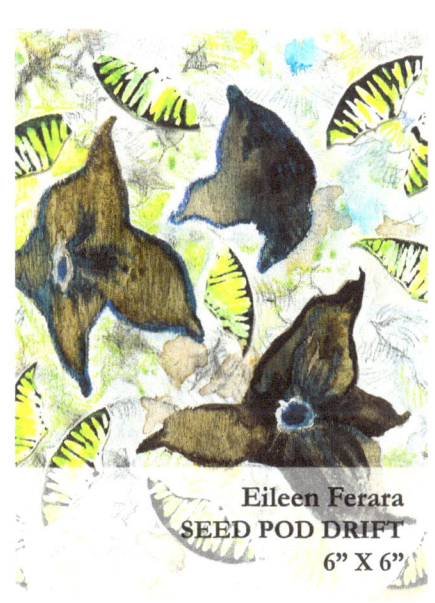

Eileen Ferara
SEED POD DRIFT
6" X 6"

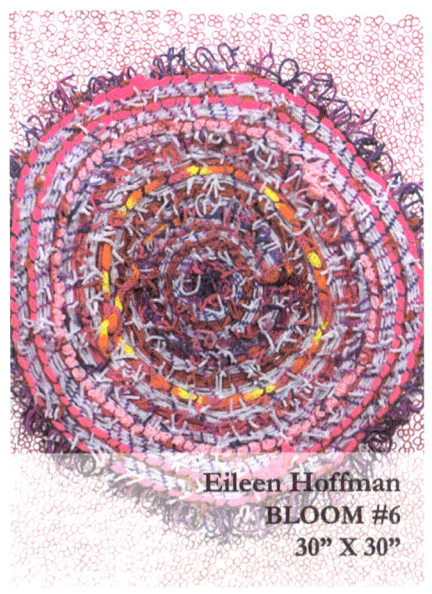

Eileen Hoffman
BLOOM #6
30" X 30"

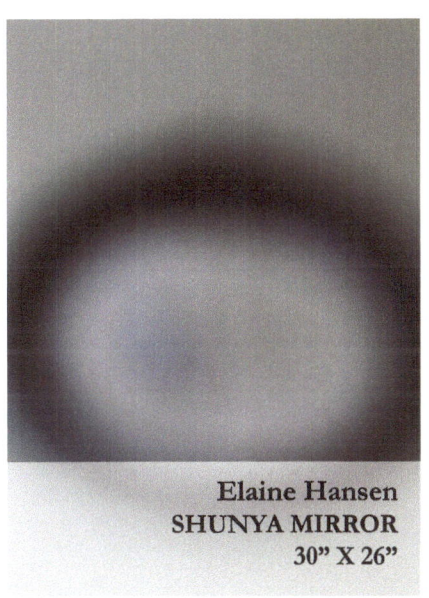

Elaine Hansen
SHUNYA MIRROR
30" X 26"

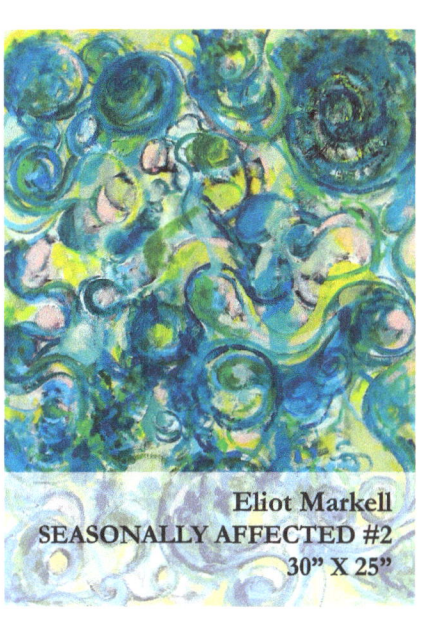

Eliot Markell
SEASONALLY AFFECTED #2
30" X 25"

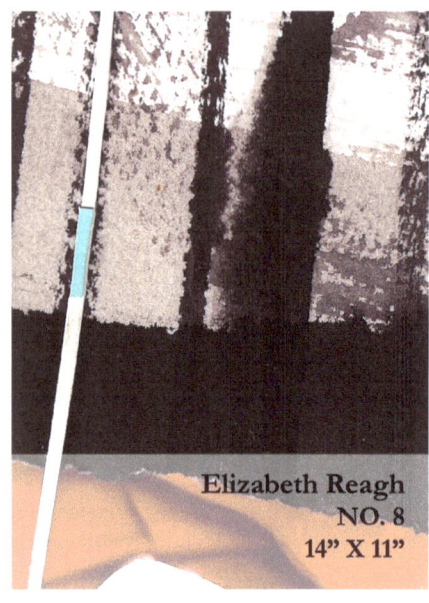

Elizabeth Reagh
NO. 8
14" X 11"

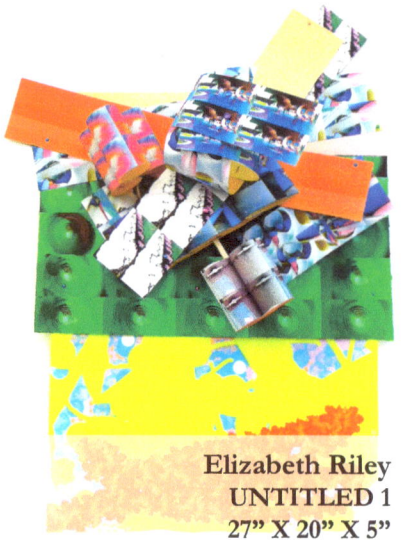

Elizabeth Riley
UNTITLED 1
27" X 20" X 5"

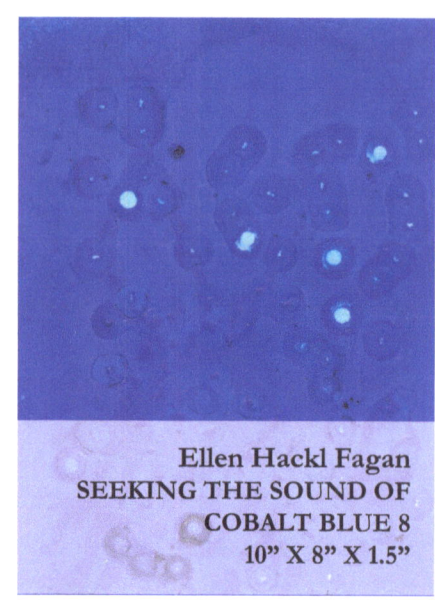

Ellen Hackl Fagan
SEEKING THE SOUND OF
COBALT BLUE 8
10" X 8" X 1.5"

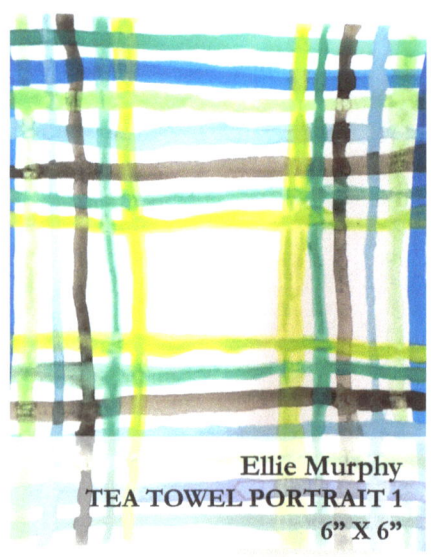

Ellie Murphy
TEA TOWEL PORTRAIT 1
6" X 6"

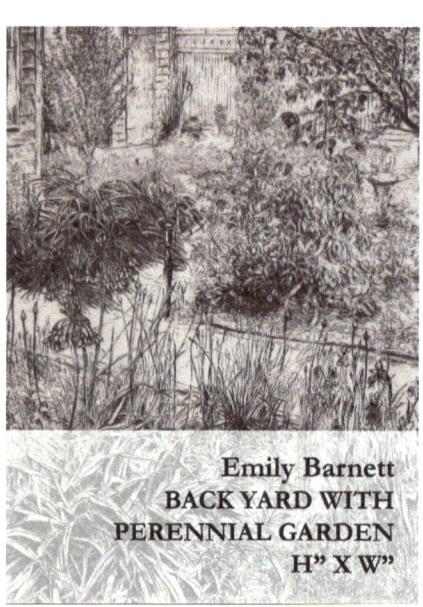

Emily Barnett
BACK YARD WITH
PERENNIAL GARDEN
H" X W"

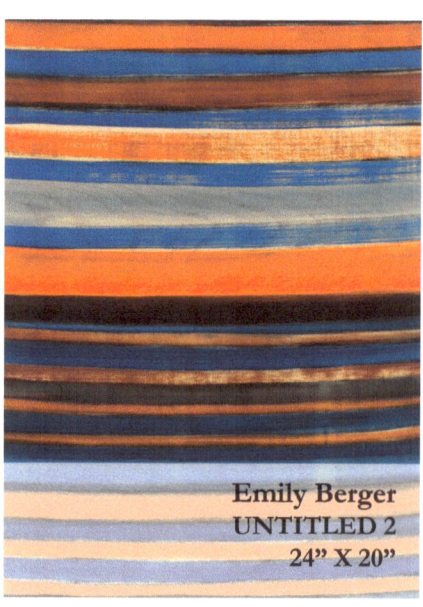

Emily Berger
UNTITLED 2
24" X 20"

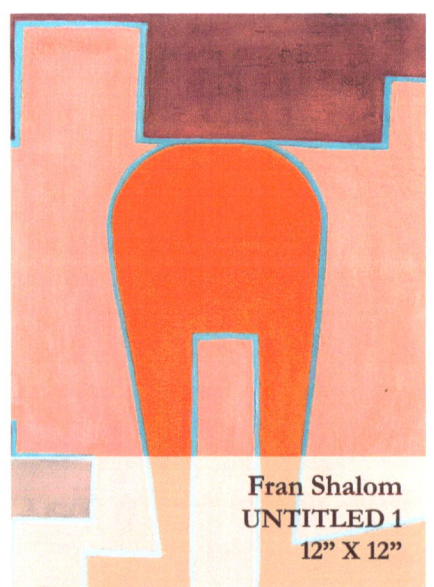

Fran Shalom
UNTITLED 1
12" X 12"

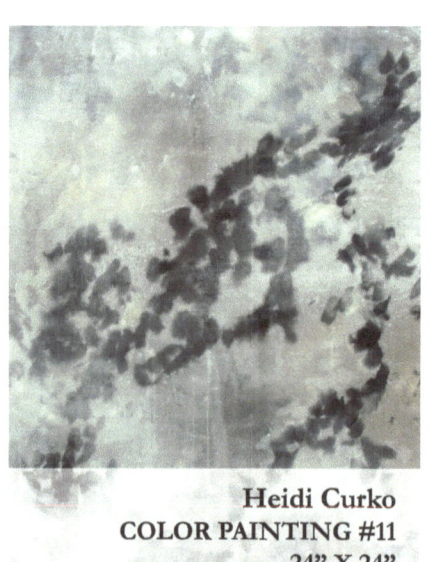

Heidi Curko
COLOR PAINTING #11
24" X 24"

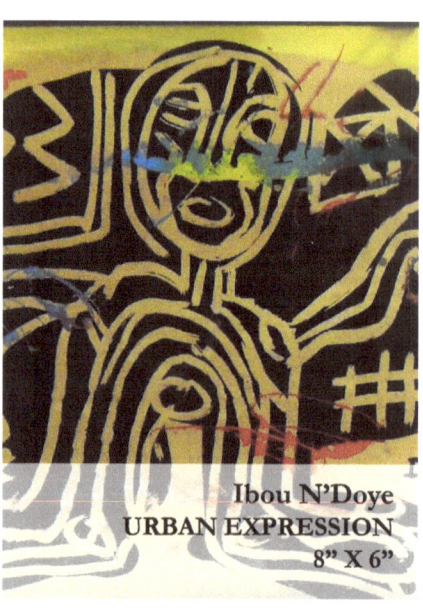

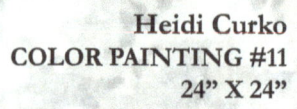

Ibou N'Doye
URBAN EXPRESSION
8" X 6"

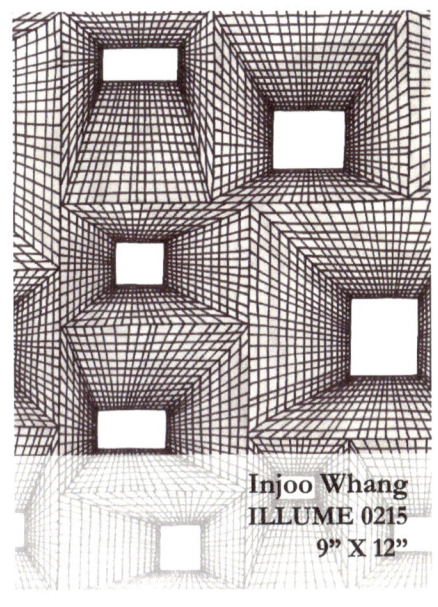

Injoo Whang
ILLUME 0215
9" X 12"

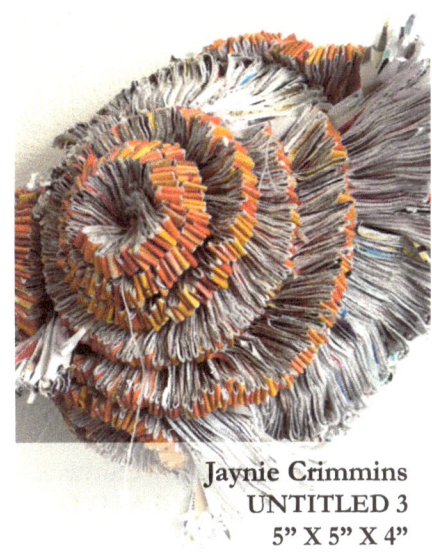

Jaynie Crimmins
UNTITLED 3
5" X 5" X 4"

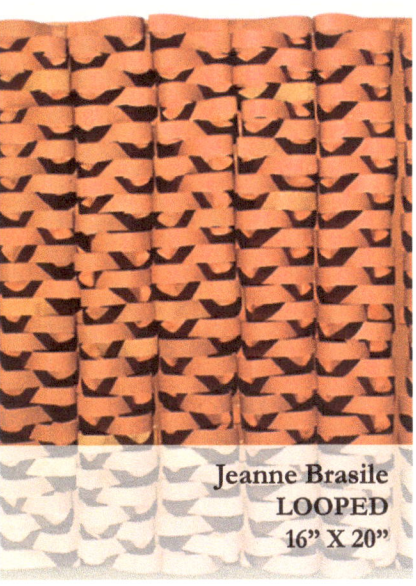

Jeanne Brasile
LOOPED
16" X 20"

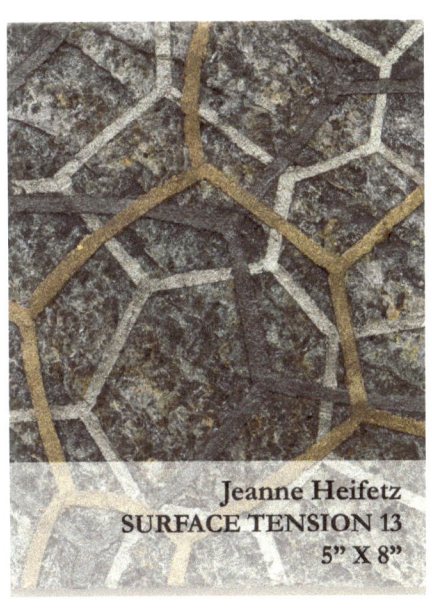

Jeanne Heifetz
SURFACE TENSION 13
5" X 8"

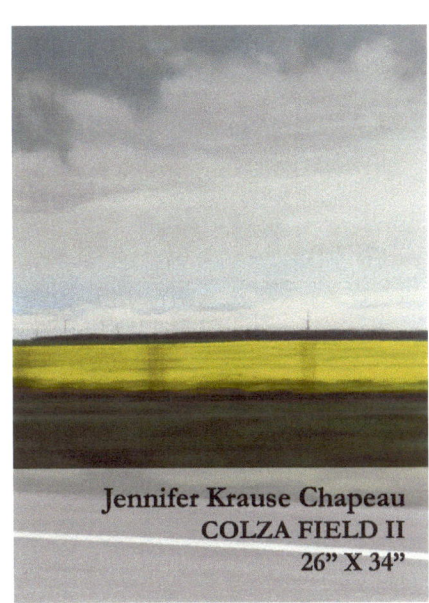

Jennifer Krause Chapeau
COLZA FIELD II
26" X 34"

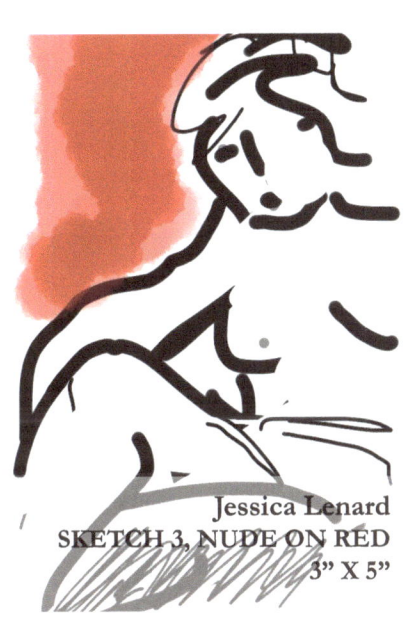

Jessica Lenard
SKETCH 3, NUDE ON RED
3" X 5"

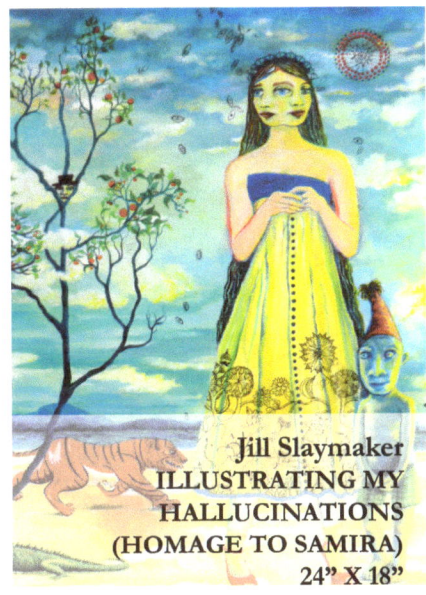

Jill Slaymaker
ILLUSTRATING MY
HALLUCINATIONS
(HOMAGE TO SAMIRA)
24" X 18"

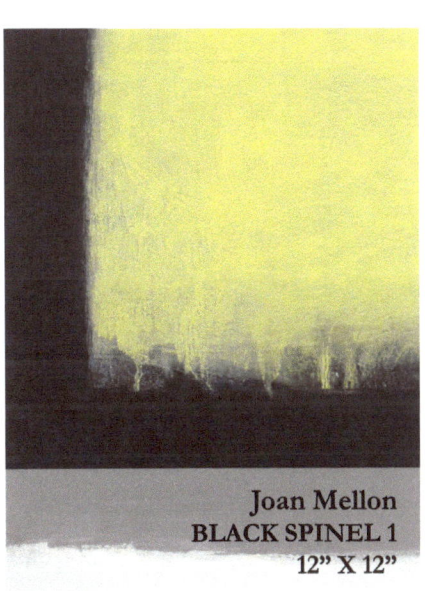

Joan Mellon
BLACK SPINEL 1
12" X 12"

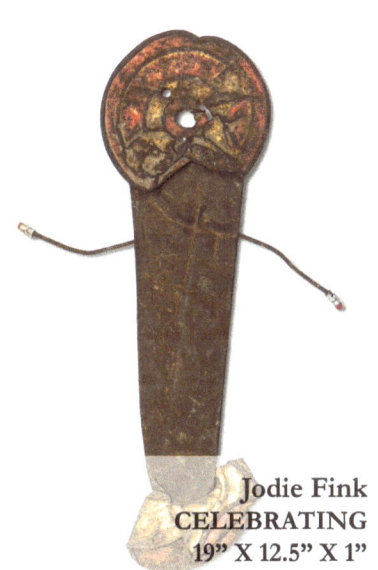

Jodie Fink
CELEBRATING
19" X 12.5" X 1"

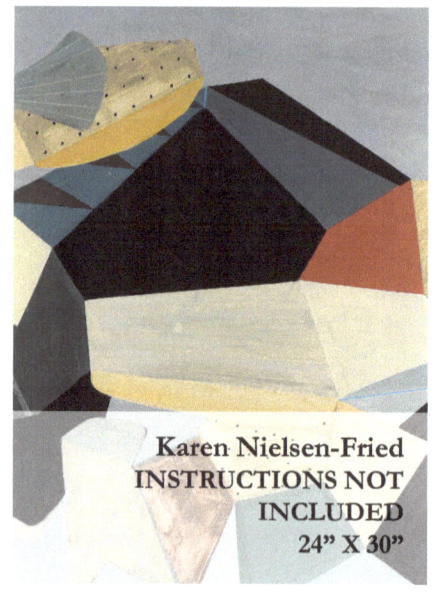

Karen Nielsen-Fried
INSTRUCTIONS NOT
INCLUDED
24" X 30"

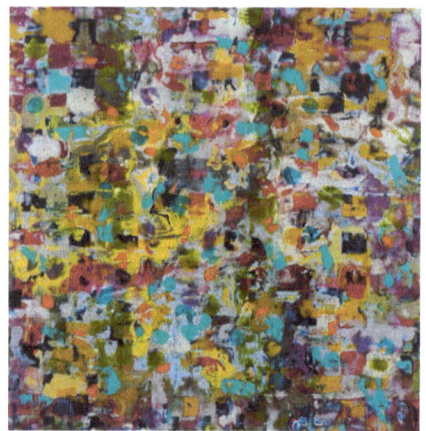

Kathy Cantwell
RELATIVITY
24" X 24"

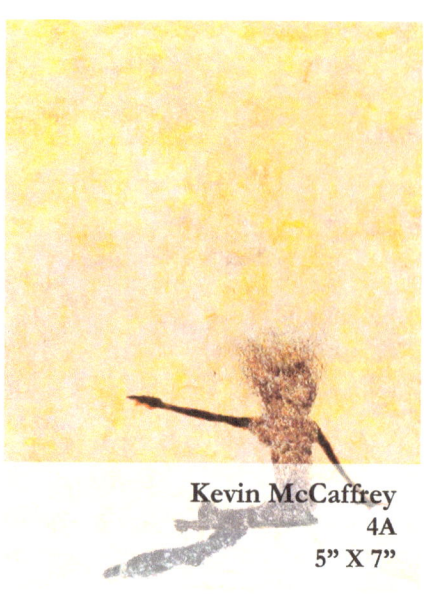

Kevin McCaffrey
4A
5" X 7"

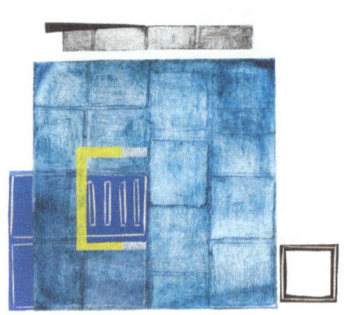

Leslie Kerby
CONTAINMENT USU20GP
15.5" X 17"

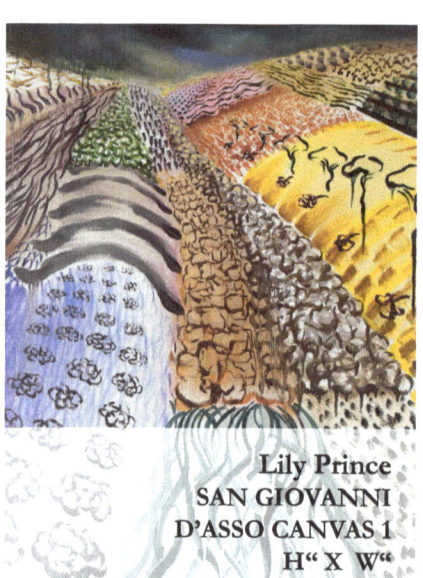
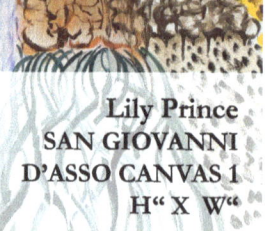

Lily Prince
SAN GIOVANNI
D'ASSO CANVAS 1
H" X W"

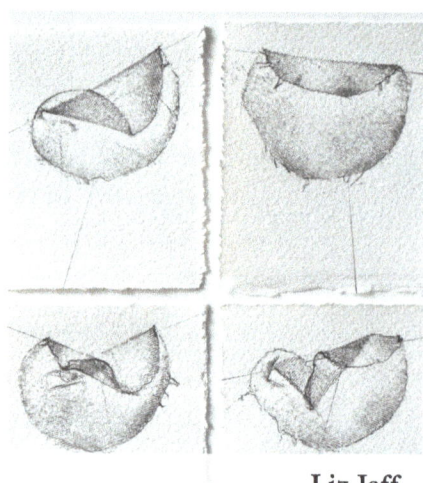

Liz Jaff
SINGLEFOLD 10
3.5" X 2.75"

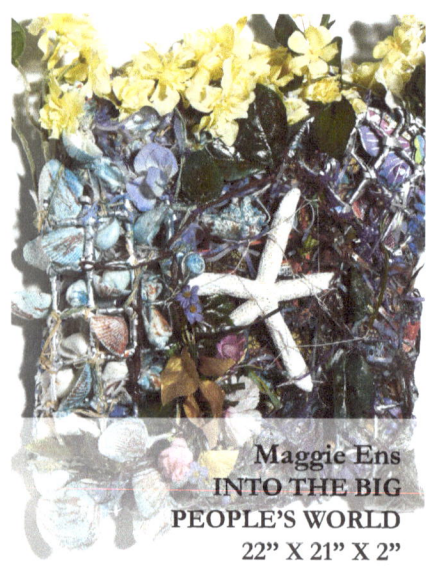

Maggie Ens
INTO THE BIG
PEOPLE'S WORLD
22" X 21" X 2"

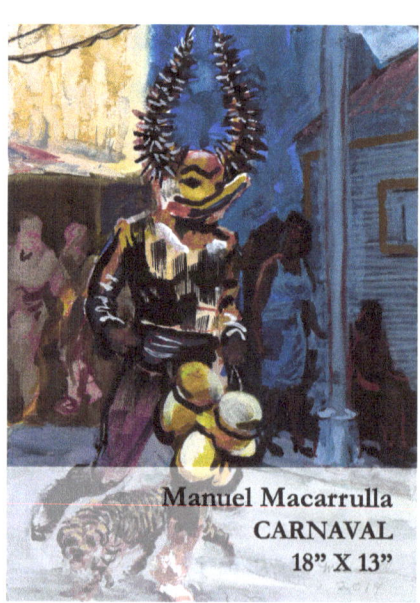

Manuel Macarrulla
CARNAVAL
18" X 13"

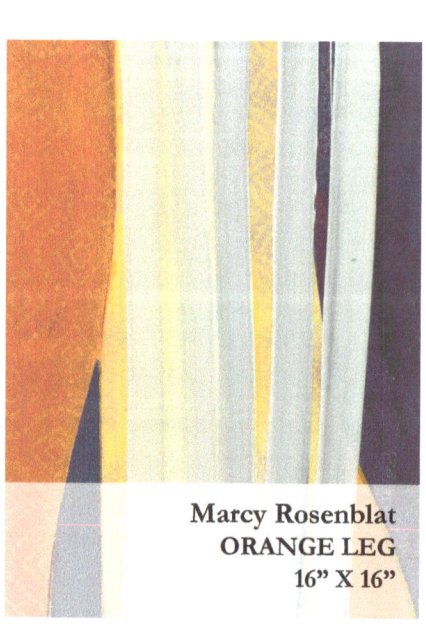

Marcy Rosenblat
ORANGE LEG
16" X 16"

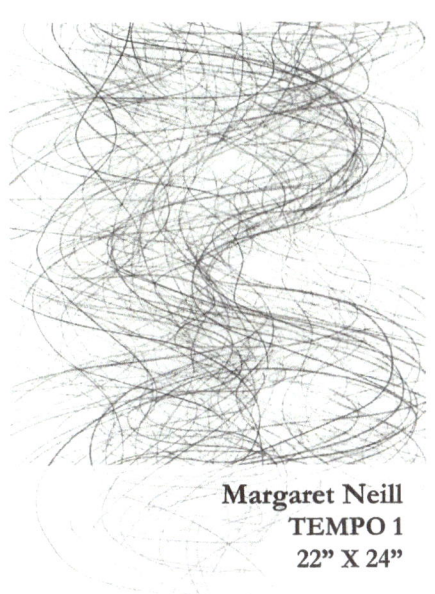

Margaret Neill
TEMPO 1
22" X 24"

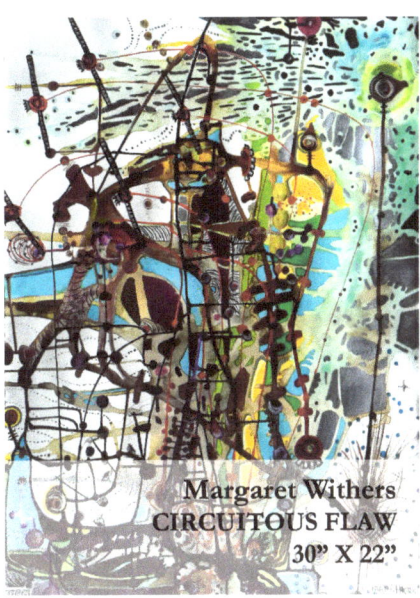

Margaret Withers
CIRCUITOUS FLAW
30" X 22"

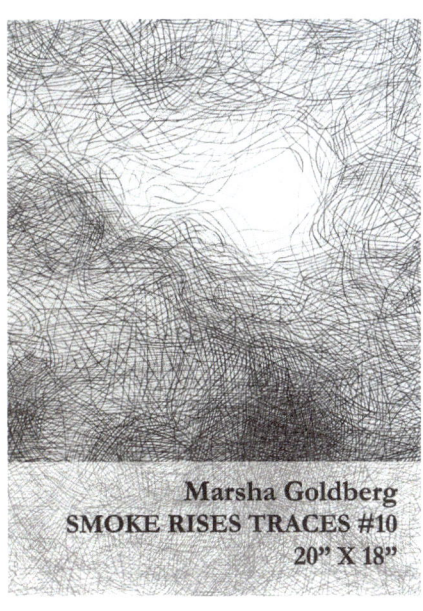

Marsha Goldberg
SMOKE RISES TRACES #10
20" X 18"

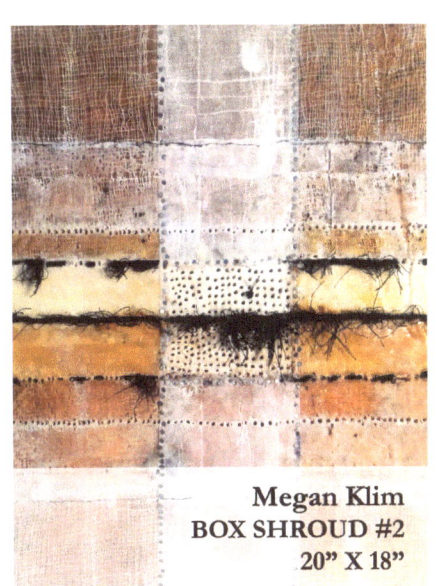

Megan Klim
BOX SHROUD #2
20" X 18"

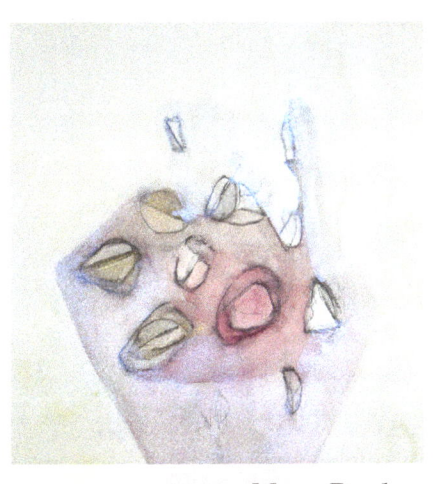

Mona Brody
GOLD
15" X 11"

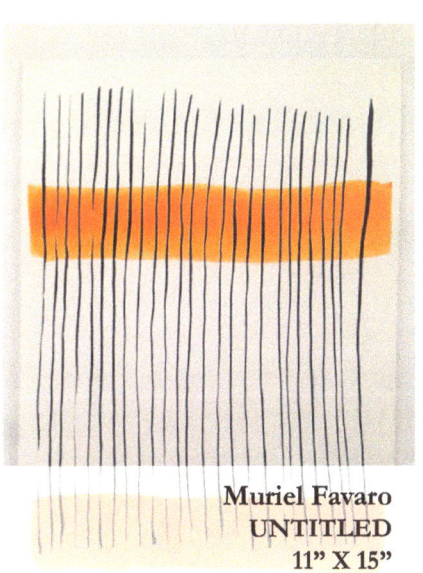

Muriel Favaro
UNTITLED
11" X 15"

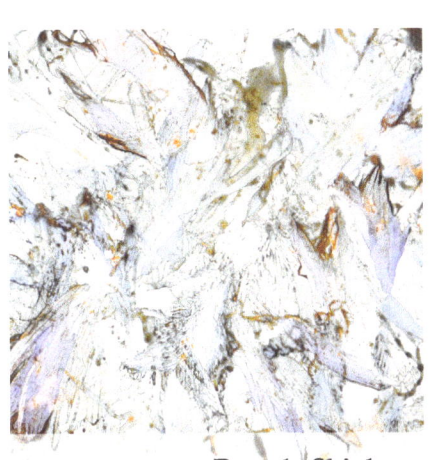

Pamela Shipley
DATA DRAWING #29
SAINT JUDE
12" X 12"

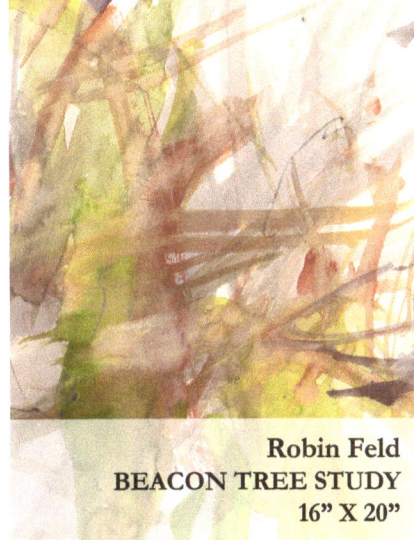

Robin Feld
BEACON TREE STUDY
16" X 20"

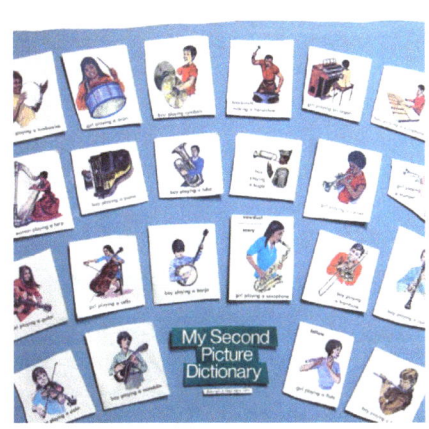

Roger Sayre
MY SECOND PICTURE
DICTIONARY
H" X W"

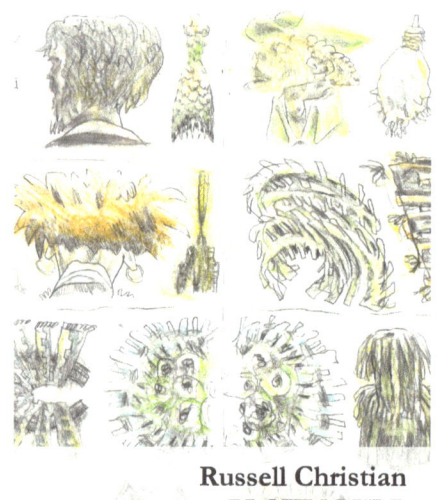

Russell Christian
BLOWN BULB
10" X 8"

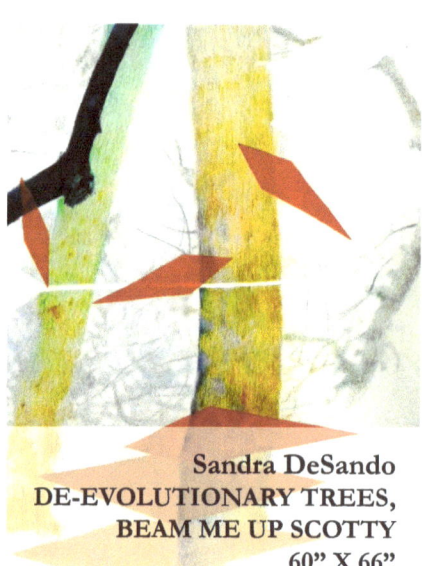

Sandra DeSando
DE-EVOLUTIONARY TREES,
BEAM ME UP SCOTTY
60" X 66"

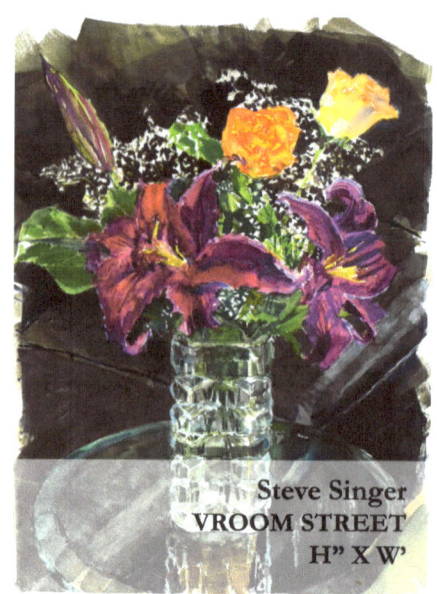

Steve Singer
VROOM STREET
H" X W'

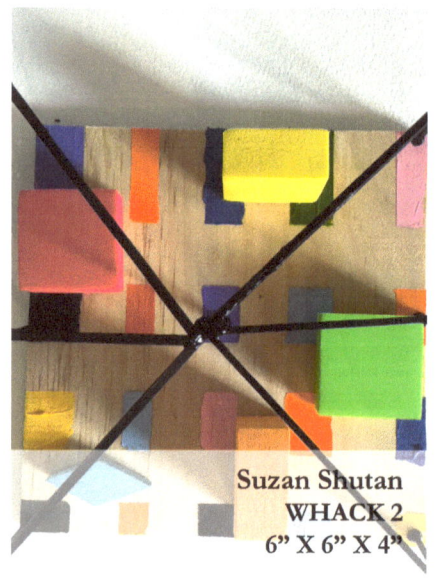

Suzan Shutan
WHACK 2
6" X 6" X 4"

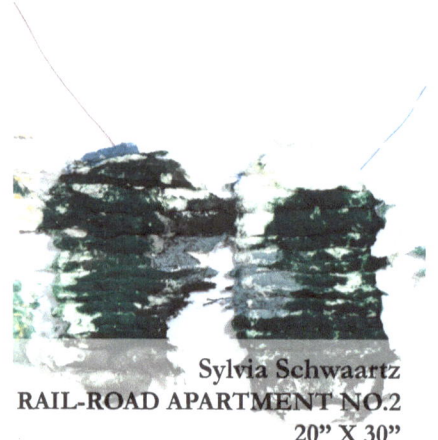

Sylvia Schwaartz
RAIL-ROAD APARTMENT NO.2
20" X 30"

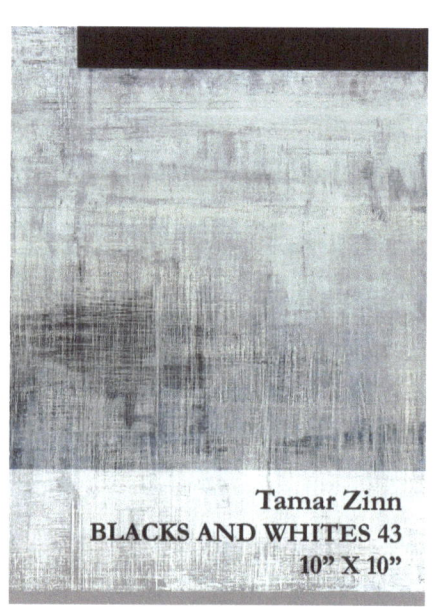

Tamar Zinn
BLACKS AND WHITES 43
10" X 10"

Tenesh Webber
RING
20" X 20"

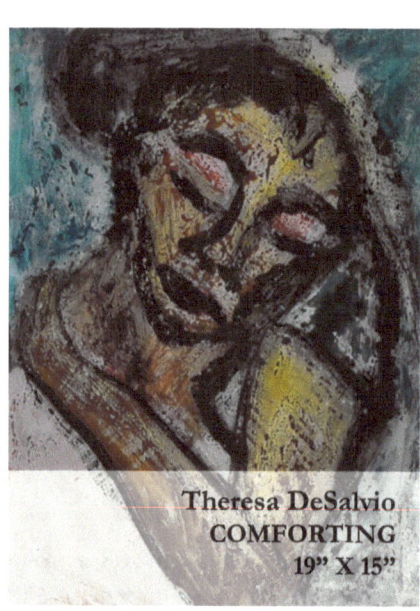

Theresa DeSalvio
COMFORTING
19" X 15"

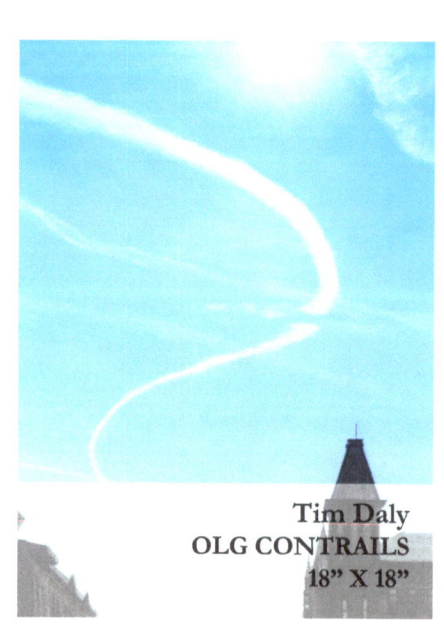

Tim Daly
OLG CONTRAILS
18" X 18"

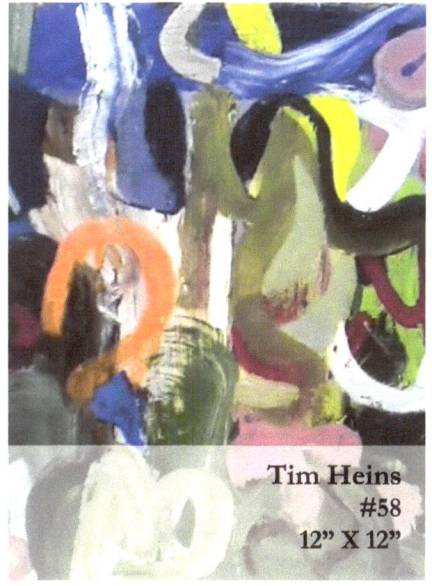

Tim Heins
#58
12" X 12"

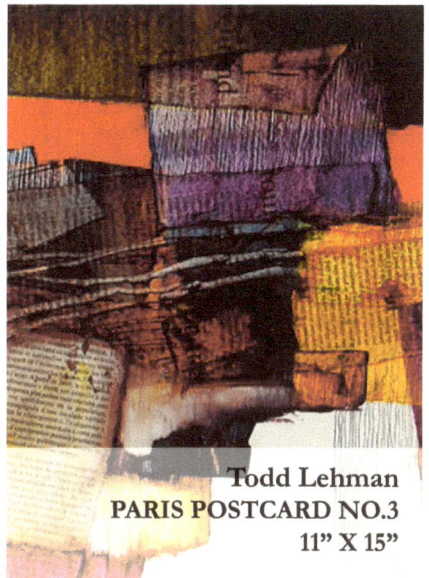

Todd Lehman
PARIS POSTCARD NO.3
11" X 15"

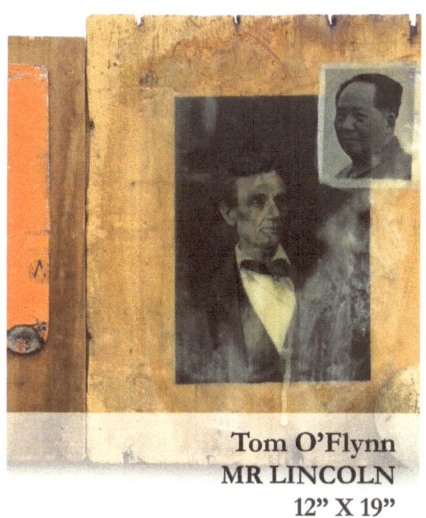

Tom O'Flynn
MR LINCOLN
12" X 19"

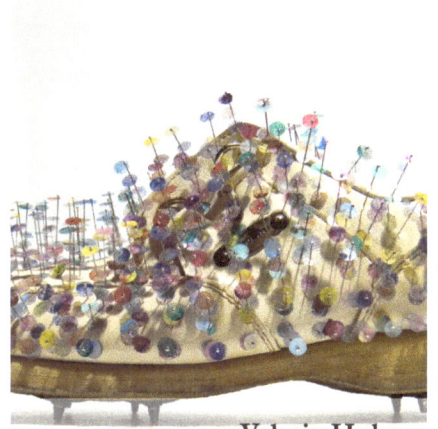

Valerie Huhn
FINGERPRINT PIN GOLF
SHOES 1 & 2
16" X 15" X 6"

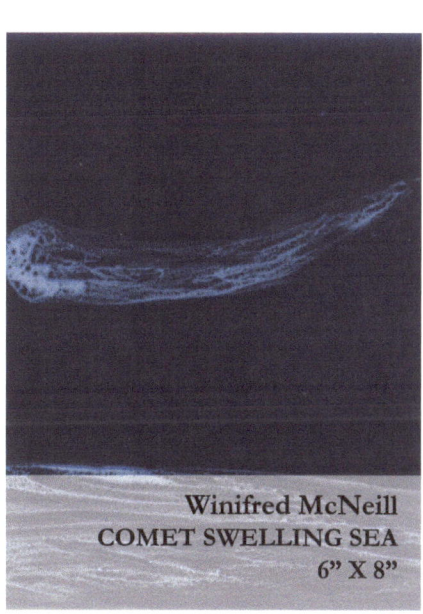

Winifred McNeill
COMET SWELLING SEA
6" X 8"

2015 marks the third annual BIG SMALL SHOW at Drawing Rooms. Our biggest exhibit of the year includes 80 artists from the NJ/NY metropolitan area. Our goal is to create a show with a large array of innovative and exceptional new paintings, drawings and 3-dimensional works to produce an exhibition that surveys recent art in our area.

For THE BIG SMALL SHOW we make full use of our multi-gallery room format to gather a group of small works from each artist, grouping them in context together with one another, creating visual, formal and conceptual connections, amplifying themes and deepening ways of understanding the works.

Curator Anne Trauben has included new artists to this exhibition, as well as artists whose work we exhibit throughout the year work. Many of the artists in the show, as well as other artists invited from within the community, have generously donated a work to the Silent Auction at the Fundraiser Gala.

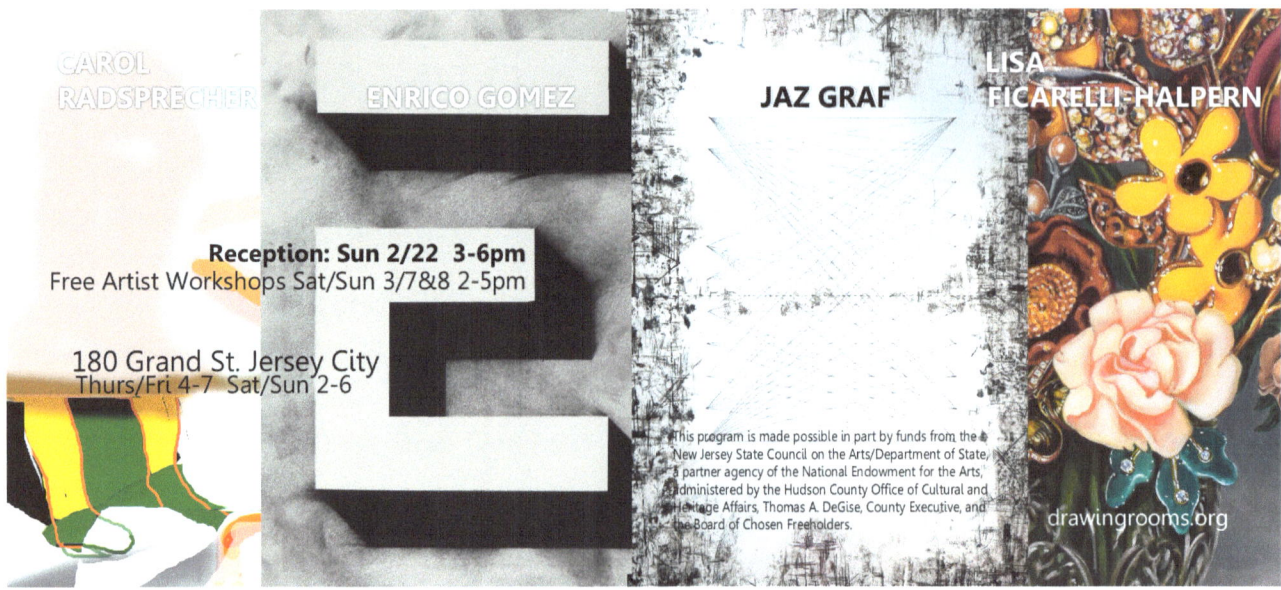

CAROL RADSPRECHER

ENRICO GOMEZ

JAZ GRAF

LISA FICARELLI-HALPERN

Reception: Sun 2/22 3-6pm
Free Artist Workshops Sat/Sun 3/7&8 2-5pm

180 Grand St. Jersey City
Thurs/Fri 4-7 Sat/Sun 2-6

This program is made possible in part by funds from the
New Jersey State Council on the Arts/Department of State,
a partner agency of the National Endowment for the Arts,
administered by the Hudson County Office of Cultural and
Heritage Affairs, Thomas A. DeGise, County Executive, and
the Board of Chosen Freeholders.

drawingrooms.org

PROJECT ROOMS
February 20th - March 15th, 2015

SUNDAY, FEBRUARY 22- RECEPTION 3-6pm

Nine solo exhibitions in drawing, painting and print featuring: Terri Amig: *Mercury and the Little Mysteries*; Enrico Gomez: *Paper Works*; Lisa Ficarelli-Halpern: *Chamber Pieces*; Eileen Ferara: *Estuary*; Jaz Graf: *In Other Words*; Carol Radsprecher: *We've Escaped the Studio!*; Eliot Markell: *Imaginary Sculptures*; James Prez: *Bird(s) on a Wire*; and Max Velez: *Faces*.

This month each room in Drawing Rooms becomes a reflection of a single artist's investigation of their experience of nature and of the nature of thought. These new sets of works by NJ/NY area artists explore the internal life by describing externals: animals, plants, landscape, people and text all become part of an internal narrative. Their work examines the natural environment as well as the very tools of narrative communication and thought, re-imagining all they see and endowing these images with meaning.

In Terri Amig's paintings, the gulls and shells and sea-life of the Jersey coast become mythic, messengers with knowledge of eternity.

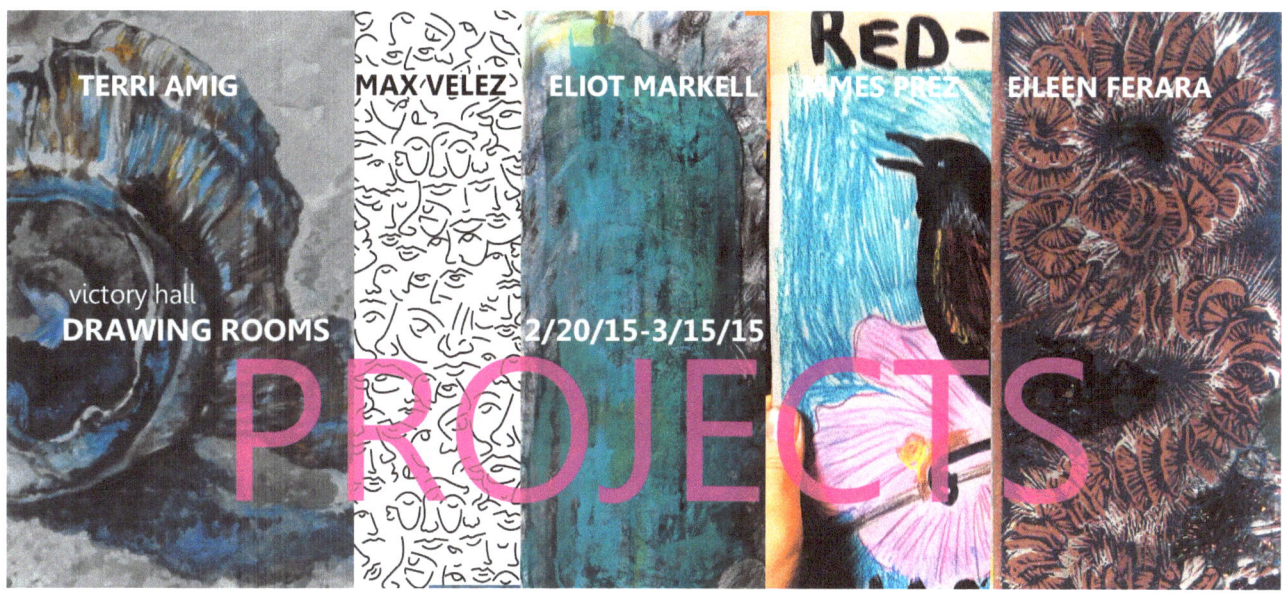

TERRI AMIG   MAX VELEZ   ELIOT MARKELL   JAMES PREZ   EILEEN FERARA

victory hall
DRAWING ROOMS   2/20/15-3/15/15   PROJECTS

James Prez' disarming drawings of birds in a faux environment recall our earliest attempts as children to depict what we considered then to be wondrous fellow-creatures.

Eliot Markell creates from nature; his drawings are nebulous and evocative forms on the verge of becoming.

Eileen Ferara's Estuary drawings pair expressive images from local waterways with text from Hemmingway's Old Man and the Sea and graphic forms, to tell a contemporary tale of life and loss.

Max Velez' Faces presents frantically active and intensely narrative drawings– a depiction of the workings of his mind filled with text, self images, memories and beautiful natural structures.

In contrast, Enrico Gomez' PaperWorks present written language and graphic letter-forms in a way that is ordered and precise, and yet are dissolved into a flood of saturated color.

Lisa Ficarelli-Halpern's lush, realistic oil paintings and prints employ decorative pattern that depict a cultivated image of nature, and engage and subvert familiar traditional motifs and themes.

Jaz Graf creates a wrapped and shredded installation in print and muslin in which narratives from old sketchbooks and personal journals are "eviscerated" and disclosed in a new form.

Carol Radschprecher's wildly chaotic yet playfully colorful images portray the calamity of everyday life.

The public is invited to the free artists' reception on Sunday, 2/22 from 3-6pm and to the free Artist Workshops on Saturday/Sunday, March 7th and 8th from 3-5pm, where they can meet the artists in a small-group setting to learn about their work and try out some hands-on art activities.

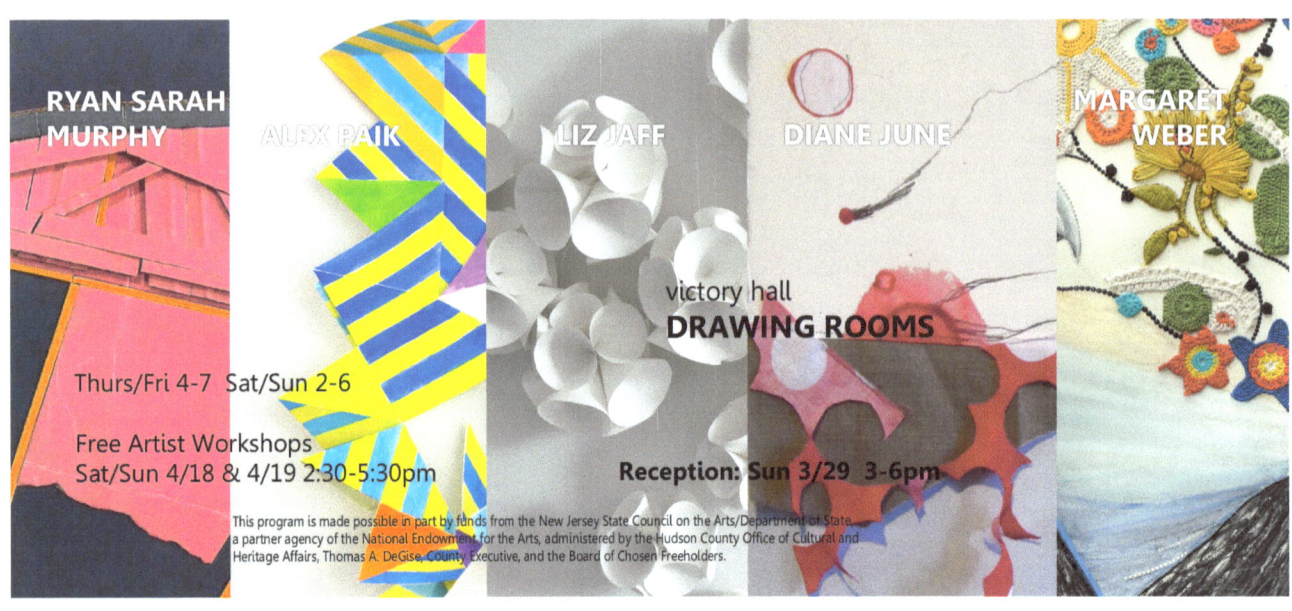

RYAN SARAH
MURPHY

ALEX PAIK

LIZ JAFF

DIANE JUNE

MARGARET
WEBER

Thurs/Fri 4-7 Sat/Sun 2-6

Free Artist Workshops
Sat/Sun 4/18 & 4/19 2:30-5:30pm

victory hall
DRAWING ROOMS

Reception: Sun 3/29 3-6pm

This program is made possible in part by funds from the New Jersey State Council on the Arts/Department of State, a partner agency of the National Endowment for the Arts, administered by the Hudson County Office of Cultural and Heritage Affairs, Thomas A. DeGise, County Executive, and the Board of Chosen Freeholders.

PAPER
CONSTRUCTIONS
March 27th - April 5th, 2015

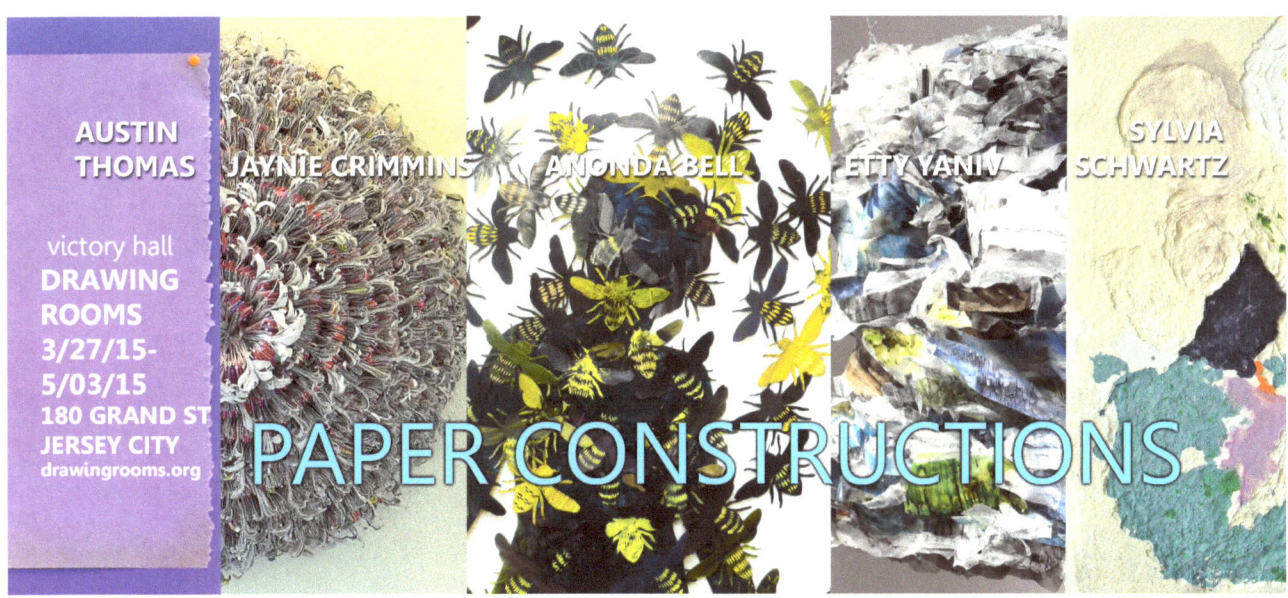

AUSTIN THOMAS

JAYNIE CRIMMINS

ANONDA BELL

ETTY YANIV

SYLVIA SCHWARTZ

victory hall
DRAWING ROOMS
3/27/15-
5/03/15
**180 GRAND ST
JERSEY CITY**
drawingrooms.org

PAPER CONSTRUCTIONS

SUNDAY, March 29 RECEPTION 3-6pm

PAPER CONSTRUCTIONS 3/27/15 - 5/3/15 features 10 artists in 9 exhibition rooms working with various types of paper– including handmade paper, recyclable paper and cardboard, among others, creating narrative and abstract sculpture, installation, drawing and different types of collage. Curated by Anne Trauben. Artists include: Etty Yaniv, Sylvia Schwartz, Jaynie Gillman Crimmins, Anonda Bell, Alex Paik, Margaret Weber, Liz Jaff, Austin Thomas, Diane Tenerelli-June and Ryan Sarah Murphy.

Paper is as basic as it comes in art. From childhood through adult, for both artists and non artists, the appeal and the immediacy of paper will always be there. Try as they might, technical devices will never replace it. Blank paper is so often the start of one's art making. Paper, as a natural material, adds another layer of meaning to the abstract and narrative aspect of many of these artists' works. Yaniv, Schwartz, Bell, Weber, Crimmins & Murphy's works speak of nature and the environment, while both Thomas and June create their own unique collage languages. Paik's connects the rhythm of music to the movement and harmony in color and shape, while Jaff uses the material to create ethereal beauty. This is a materials show and these artists love the material and know it well.

The public is invited to the free artists' reception on Sunday, 3/29 from 3-6pm and to the free Artist Workshops on Saturday/Sunday, April 18th and 19th from 2:30-5:30pm, where they can meet the artists in a small-group setting to learn about their work and try out some hands-on art activities.

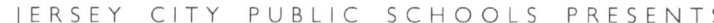

TEACHER *as* ARTiST

Drawing Rooms 180 Grand Street
Jersey City, NJ 07302
Opening Reception: Thursday May 7, 5:00-7:00PM

The exhibit is open to the public May 6-10.
Thursday/Friday 4:00-7:00PM
Saturday/Sunday 2:00-6:00PM

For further information, please contact
Ms. Ann Marley, Supervisor, Visual & Media Arts, JCPS
at 201.915.6038 or amarley@jcboe.org

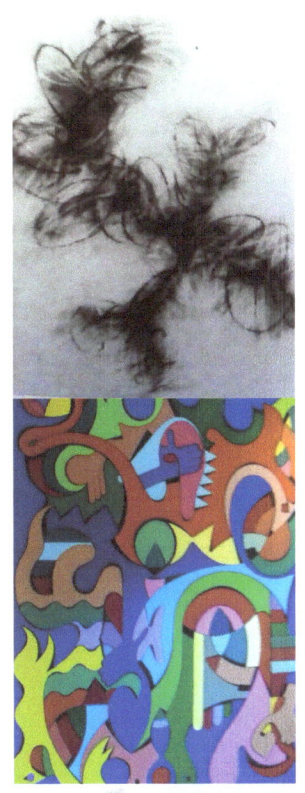

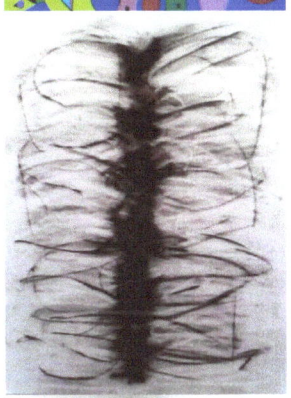

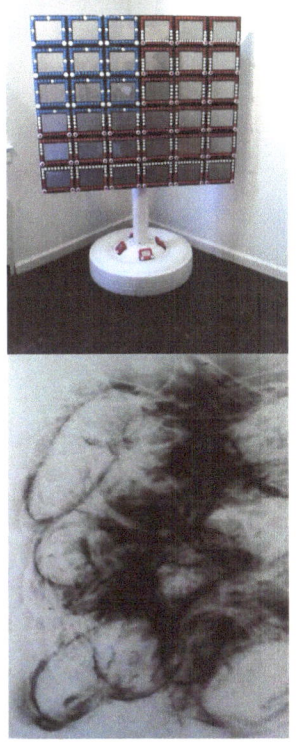

TEACHER AS ARTIST
May 6th - May 10th, 2015

Featuring drawing, painting and sculpture from 22 of Jersey City's public school Teaching Artists who diligently and creatively strive to build the aesthetic character of their students, while maintaining their own artistic practices. This exhibition, curated by Heidi Curko, celebrates the creation of Jersey City Teaching Artist's own artworks.

Artists:
Janice Quarto,

Alexis Martinez,

Jennifer Tiongsen,

Gregory Charles,

John Bradford,

Carolyn Frazier,

Julia Difeo,

Jessica Ward,

Patricia Chumpitaz,

Daniel Marck,

Michael Markman,

Hope Taylor,

Diana Gonzales,

Barbara Williams,

Tony Noguiera,

Ralph Pyrzanowski,

Heidi Curko,

Maria Francisco,

Kristen Marino,

Pamela Brown,

Rossana Villaflor,

Marina Samuels

Artist Reception on Thursday, 5/7/15 from 5p - 7p.

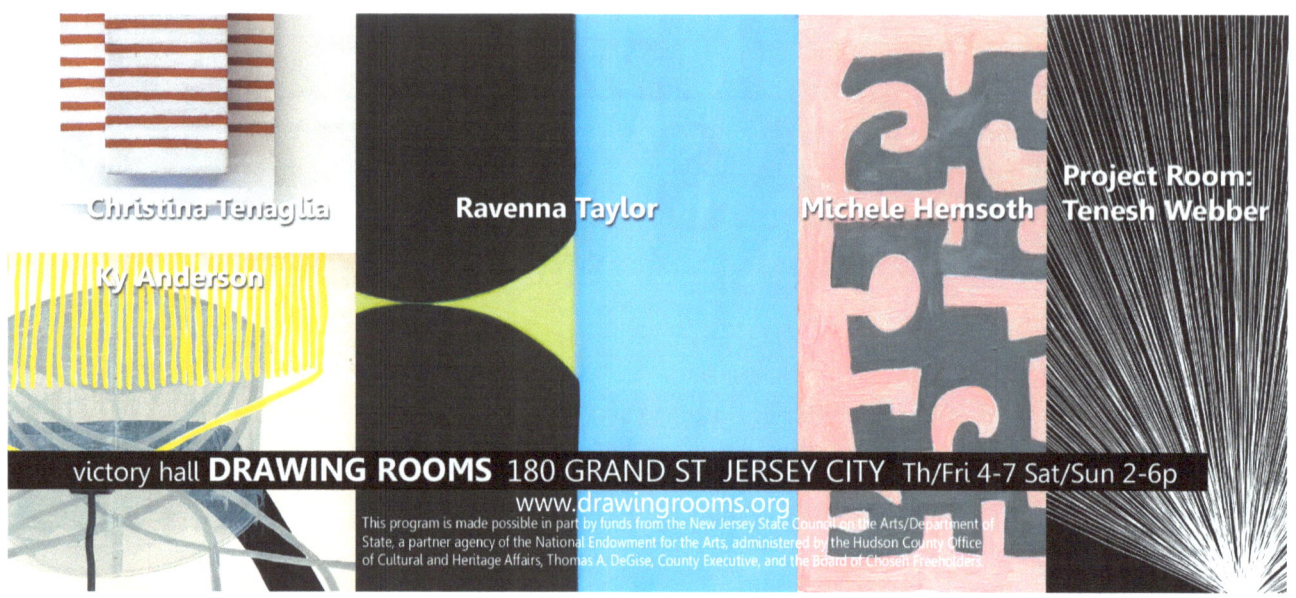

Christina Tenaglia

Ky Anderson

Ravenna Taylor

Michele Hemsoth

Project Room:
Tenesh Webber

victory hall **DRAWING ROOMS** 180 GRAND ST JERSEY CITY Th/Fri 4-7 Sat/Sun 2-6p
www.drawingrooms.org
This program is made possible in part by funds from the New Jersey State Council on the Arts/Department of State, a partner agency of the National Endowment for the Arts, administered by the Hudson County Office of Cultural and Heritage Affairs, Thomas A. DeGise, County Executive, and the Board of Chosen Freeholders.

LITTLE HAND

May 22nd - June 28th, 2015

Little Hand:
quirky
bashful / bold
naive
odd
childlike but sophisticated
organic forms/shapes that are animated
humourous
drawn by hand
hand is significant
take on a personality
secret narrative
familiar but not specific

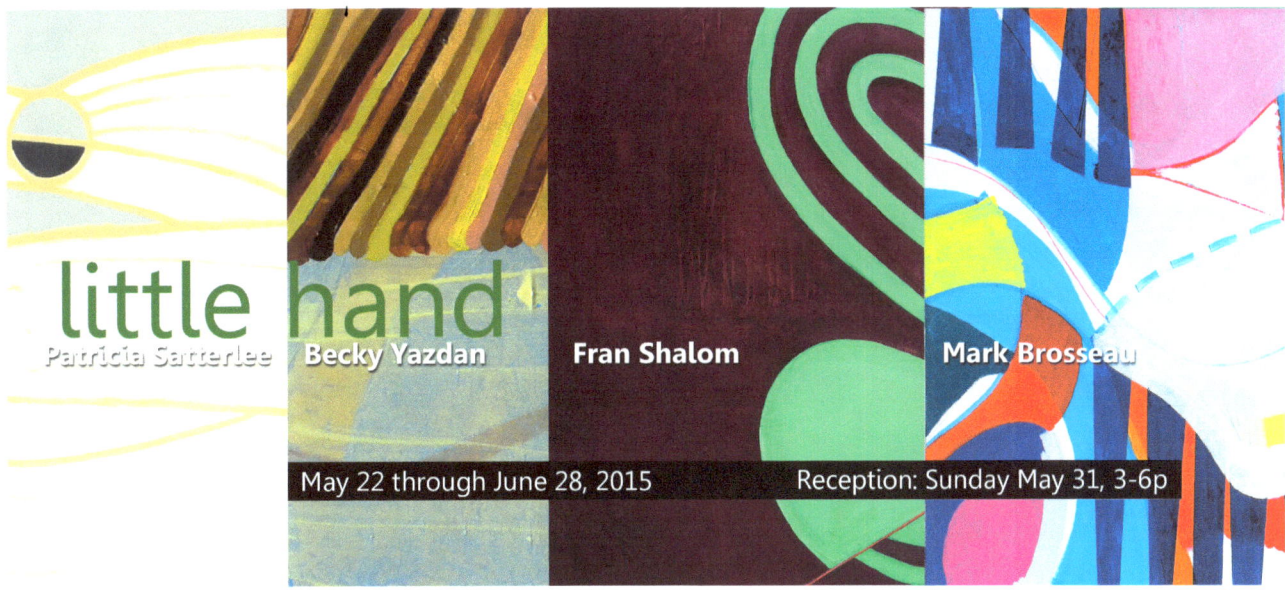

little hand

Patricia Satterlee   Becky Yazdan   Fran Shalom   Mark Brosseau

May 22 through June 28, 2015   Reception: Sunday May 31, 3-6p

Works in Painting, Drawing and Sculpture by Christina Tenaglia, Ravenna Taylor, Mark Brosseau,Fran Shalom, Patricia Satterlee, Michele Hemsoth, Becky Yazdan, Ky Anderson.

Special Project Room: Tenesh Webber photograms

Reception: Sunday May 31, 3-6pm

Eight artists creating organic and animated abstracted painting, drawing and sculpture,each in their own way. Drawing from a pop sensibility, a lil' humor, kinda awkward and bashful (yet at time same time also bold & confident) with a bit of a quirk factor- these 2d and 3d works seem familiar, yet they are not and allude to a narrative, yet there is no narrative. (Does this unique imagery come from a sort of collective unconscious?) What we've got here is a new language of abstraction that's being explored, invented and extended.

Special Project Room features Tenesh Weber's black & white Photograms: Drawing-like images from objects the artist makes in the studio, out of thread, marker on plexi, and paper.

The public is invited to the free artists' reception on Sunday, 5/31 from 3-6pm and to the free Artist Workshops on Saturday/Sunday, June 13th and 14th from 2:30-5:30pm, where they can meet the artists in a small-group setting to learn about their work and try out some hands-on art activities.

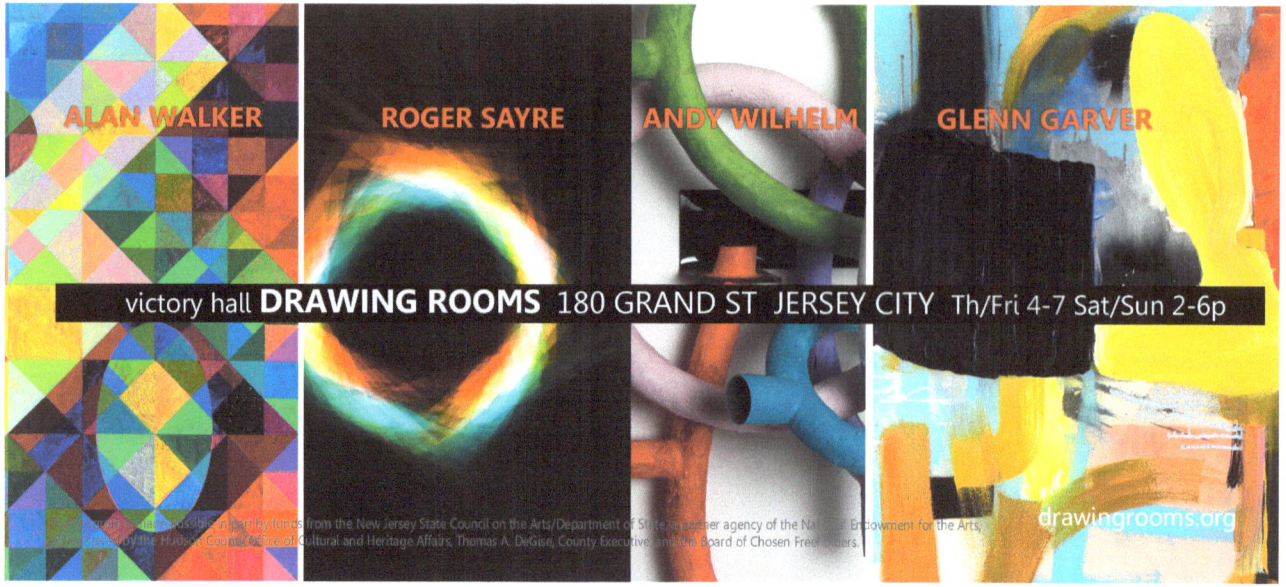

ALAN WALKER   ROGER SAYRE   ANDY WILHELM   GLENN GARVER

victory hall **DRAWING ROOMS** 180 GRAND ST JERSEY CITY Th/Fri 4-7 Sat/Sun 2-6p

drawingrooms.org

COLOR RULES

July 11th - August 16th, 2015

COLOR RULES: An exhibition engaging the expression, experience and impact of color. Nine gallery rooms featuring painting, drawing, collage, photography, sculpture and installation by Alan Walker, Andy Wilhelm, Dana Kane, Ellen Hackl Fagan, Ellie Murphy, Glenn Garver, Marianne DeAngelis, Meg Atkinson and Roger Sayre. Paintings on paper by Doug Holst in "The Tenth Room" Gallery Shop.

Opening Reception Saturday, July 11, 3pm to 6pm, Free.
July 11 through August 16,
Open Thursdays and Fridays 4 to 7pm Saturdays and Sundays 2 to 6pm.

Color is described as the property possessed by an object that produces different sensations on the eye as a result of the way the object reflects or emits light. From the earliest paintings til the present: the meaning and symbolism of early Christian art, Impressionism in the 1800s, the Fauves and Color Field painters of the 20th century - artists have been forever fascinated by color- and not just painters, of course. Current artists are engaging color in sculpture and installation to stunning effect.

Alan Walker's colorful paintings are based on geometry and color has always been his prime inspiration in art making. Alan makes his works with a destination in mind and sets up rules, but quickly finds his limits were wrong.

Andy Wilhelm's color marks both time and space. In his sculptural works, color complements, vibrates and creates an energy. Andy often allows a random process to dictate his choices and doesn't box himself in to following any rules.

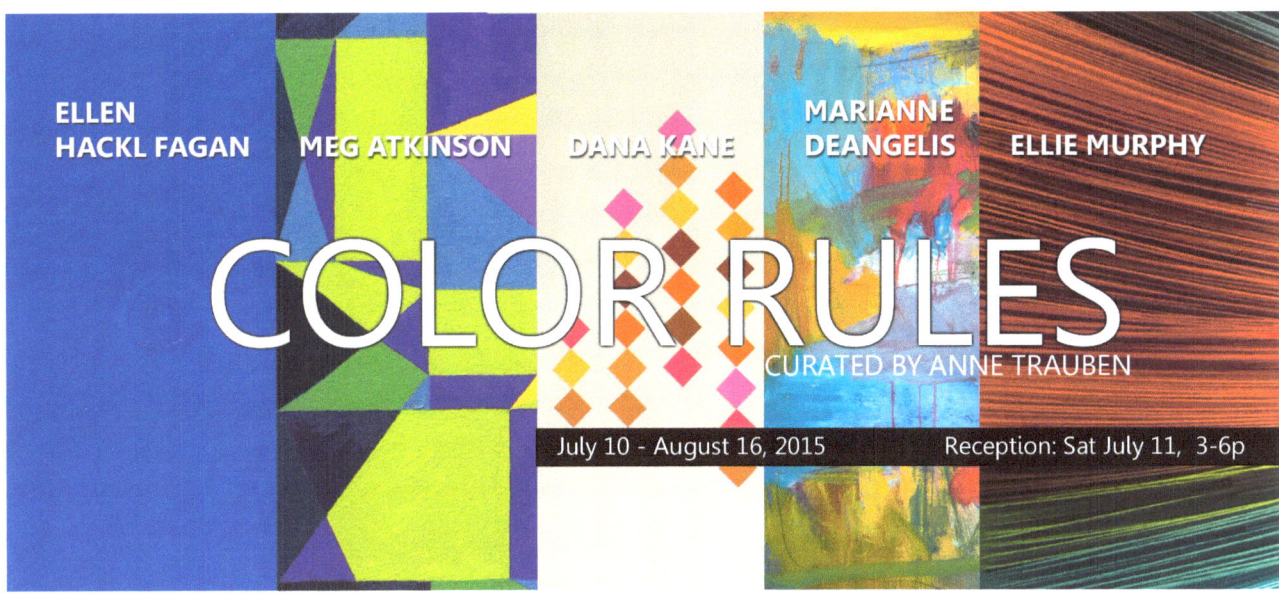

ELLEN HACKL FAGAN   **MEG ATKINSON**   **DANA KANE**   **MARIANNE DEANGELIS**   **ELLIE MURPHY**

COLOR RULES

CURATED BY ANNE TRAUBEN

July 10 - August 16, 2015   Reception: Sat July 11, 3-6p

Meg Atkinson's paintings also explore geometric abstraction. Her interest in color began as a way to flatten three-dimensionality. Meg describes her fearless process as completely rule bound.

Ellen Hackl Fagan's blue paintings create a bridge that joins color to sound and her intention is to build a universal synaesthetic language.

Dana Kane began working with color paint swatches because she wanted to understand color. Dana uses color in an intuitive way and describes her process as a sort of meditation. Her intention is to create an optical experience in the form of a rhythm and pulse that bounces the viewer's eye across the work in an "even manner".

As a sculptor, Ellie Murphy is interested in color that already exists, rather than making it as a painter does. Her color includes that which she finds, arranges, plans and controls. Ellie's yarn installation, arranged in four corners of the room, relates to the four seasons.

Marianne DeAngelis believes color evokes memories and she understands color as a language which affects the conscious and subconscious. Marianne says her intention is to use color in a truthful way. Relying on intuition, spontaneity and improvisation, Marianne is interested in exploring how a subtle shift of color can drastically change the light, space and/or flow of an entire painting.

Roger Sayre's interest in color began by creating photographic test swatches - a sort of Pantone book for himself of different color combinations. Working in a systematic way, each piece leads Roger to the next one - he makes one, studies it and decides what he likes and dislikes about it, and then makes the next pieced based on that information.

The public is invited to the free artists' reception on Sunday, 3/29 from 3-6pm and to the free Artist Workshops on Saturday/Sunday, April 18th and 19th from 2:30-5:30pm, where they can meet the artists in a small-group setting to learn about their work and try out some hands-on art activities.

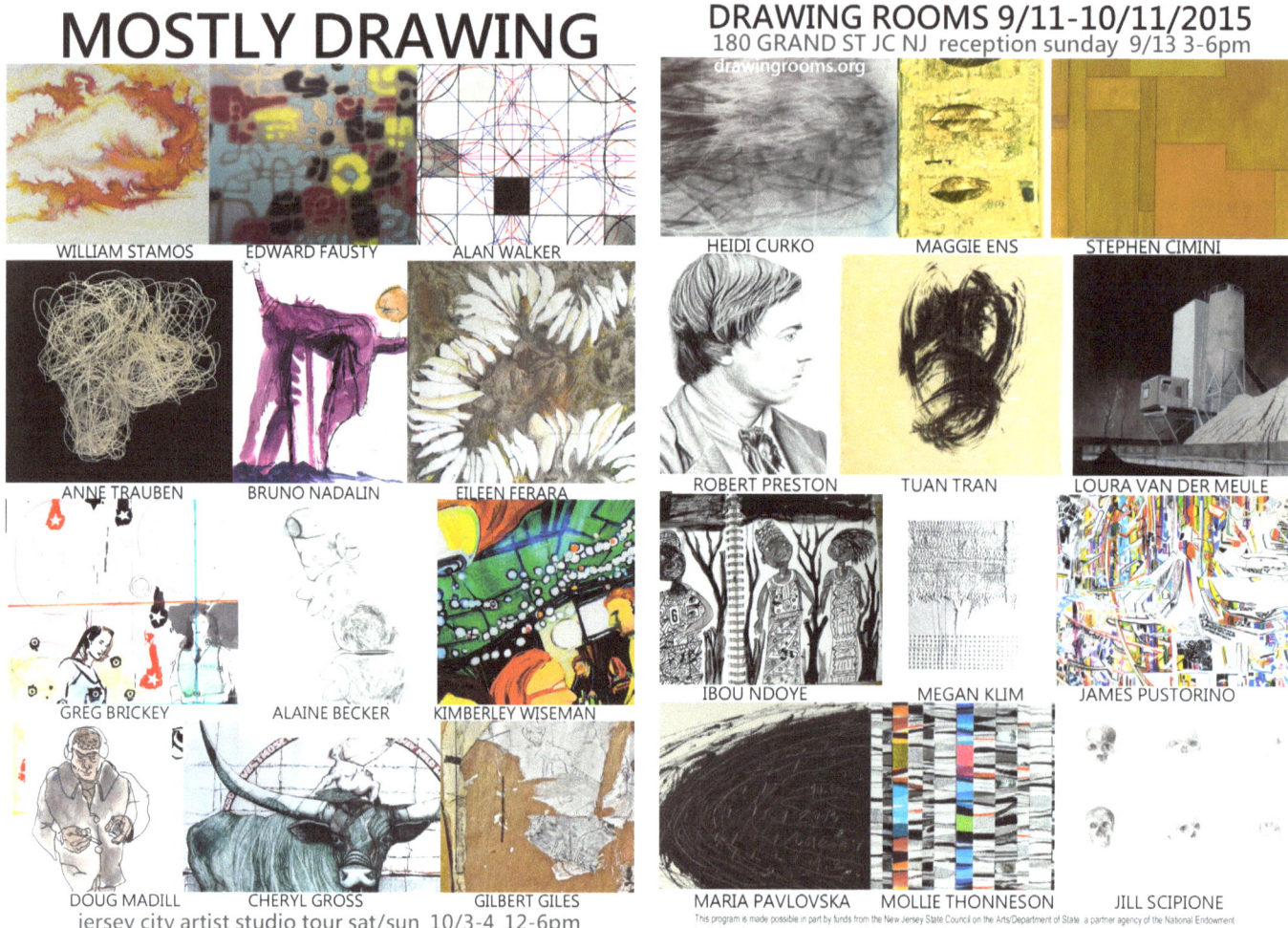

MOSTLY DRAWING

DRAWING ROOMS 9/11-10/11/2015
180 GRAND ST JC NJ reception sunday 9/13 3-6pm
drawingrooms.org

WILLIAM STAMOS   EDWARD FAUSTY   ALAN WALKER

HEIDI CURKO   MAGGIE ENS   STEPHEN CIMINI

ANNE TRAUBEN   BRUNO NADALIN   EILEEN FERARA

ROBERT PRESTON   TUAN TRAN   LOURA VAN DER MEULE

GREG BRICKEY   ALAINE BECKER   KIMBERLEY WISEMAN

IBOU NDOYE   MEGAN KLIM   JAMES PUSTORINO

DOUG MADILL   CHERYL GROSS   GILBERT GILES

jersey city artist studio tour sat/sun 10/3-4 12-6pm

MARIA PAVLOVSKA   MOLLIE THONNESON   JILL SCIPIONE

This program is made possible in part by funds from the New Jersey State Council on the Arts/Department of State, a partner agency of the National Endowment for the Arts, administered by the Hudson County Office of Cultural and Heritage Affairs. Thomas A. DeGise, County Executive, and the Board of Chosen Freeholders.

MOSTLY DRAWING
September 11th - October 10th, 2015

MOSTLY DRAWING Jersey City, 9/11/15 -10/11/15, curated by Anne Trauben and Jim Pustorino
Opening Reception Sunday, September 13, 3pm to 6pm, Free.
MOSTLY DRAWING Jersey City will be up during Jersey City Artist Studio Tour Weekend 10/3/15 & 10/4/15.

At Drawing Rooms we see the act of drawing and principles of drawing as essential to not only drawing on paper, but to painting, sculpture and even at times photography. Artists are always seeking to expand their visual language and express their message in unique ways.

This gathering of works by artists involved in the Jersey City area offers twenty-five approaches to drawing and drawing-related paintings, photographic images and three-dimensional drawing.

Robert Preston's forceful drawings of Lincoln, conspiracists and confederate generals based on the the conspiracy to assassinate Abraham Lincoln. Greg Brickey's multiple panels resemble pop/comic strip imagery but explore "ambivalence, identity, loss, and instability."

Vietnamese artist Tuan Tran's "Portraits" are a series of bold, calligraphic gestures in black paint with mother-of-pearl for an opalescent, glow that is matched by Mollie Thonneson's luminesce reassembled strips of colored drawing and writing inspired Sanskrit devotional books.

Doug Madill sketches from observation in urban streets, subways, cafes. He cites his love of observation and the spontaneity of the impromptu as inspiration for the cartoonish mode of execution in his sketches. Alan Walker presents a short retrospective of drawing over the years, ranging from his investigations of the 45 caliber gun, to a dark vision of the river surrounding Manhattan, to the schematic, mathematic, ritual-like drawing for his current abstract color works. William Stamos' tiny, organic-form, color drawings describe an illumined world of mystery and the hope for enlightenment- a concept that permeates all of his artwork.

In Jill Scipione's large drawings, realistically detailed skulls of historical peoples exist with gestural and volumetric forms borrowed from Renaissance painting to create a place where both have new purpose. In the same room, wire becomes the drawn line in Anne Trauben's expansive, etherial and organic form-changing 3D 'drawings' that appear to attach themselves to the wall -blurring the line between dimensions, and then a set of small paintings by Macedonian artist Maria Pavlovska in which paint and canvas become a vital, emotive tangle of writing on pages of an open journal.

Gilbert Giles and Bruno Nadalin both work in illustration at times, but their drawing here explores the graphic mark in more adventurous ways. Giles' small works become graphic notes; parts of cartoon panels, writing, stains and folds of paper overlap and overrule one another creating densely secret messages. Bruno Nadalin draws a loosely comic, at times beautifully grotesque, view of his experience and imaginations.

Loura van der Meule's stark oil crayon drawings of the harbor in her native Holland town, a place she says she must record before a coming change, is paralleled by Edward Fausty's photographic remembrances of 'drawing' from the studios, doors and even rooftops of Jersey City's 111 First St. studio building- a place where both these artists and others in the exhibit started working with one another, which was torn down ten years ago.

Alaine Becker's drawings "Seen/Unseen" are 'derived from organs and other internal structures of the body; some real and some invented.' Megan Klim, in the same gallery, creates 'drawings ' that are sculptural. Using a hand-awl, she punctures very thick paper with thousands of tiny holes.

In a gallery concerned with nature, Heidi Curko's energetic, atmospheric blur of structural pencil lines and shading, spring from her prior study of landscape. Eileen Ferara's colorful drawn and painted works are a reflection on the experiences of her walks in nature. Maggie Ens moves the two dimensional surface into 3D by collecting, collaging and recycling common discarded objects into her artworks.

Kim Wiseman painted paper pieces recreate night-life in strong wavy lines, showing us a glowy, richly-colorful world of bright lights and dark corners. Cheryl Gross' fantastically inventive imagery from her books, Z Factor, an illustrated novel, and Greetings From Karpland continue the story in graphic novel form. Two of West African born artist Ibou Ndoye's books of drawings overflowing with city-life and two of his black-outlined full-portraits on heavy brown cardboard finish the gallery.

Stephen Cimini presents a pair of sentinels- large glowing oil and cold wax paintings. In each of his works, the closely toned rectangles of orange or gold are defined by incised lines. James Pustorino's large horizontal panels of complex layered colors and linear structure, face off against Cimini's in a display of color intensity.

The Tenth Room features crisply rendered sky scenes by Tim Daly. Born in Jersey City, now active in Hoboken, Daly's pastel drawings are surprisingly realistic and evoke the experience of light and place.

THE DIVINE AND SUBLIME

October 23rd - November 22nd, 2015

THE DIVINE AND SUBLIME, 10/23/15 - 11/22/15, curated by Anne Trauben, features 8 artists in 9 gallery rooms showing drawing, painting, sculpture and installation.

Fitting for our unique gallery space, a former convent, The Divine and Sublime is an exhibition of works exploring the contemplative, consciousness, nature as a spiritual experience, and the sacred object: employing color, repetition, myth and symbol to evoke meaning.

Artists include Buhm Hong, Carole Kunstadt, Cicely Cottingham, Michael Ensminger, Pat Lay, Paula Overbay, Robyn Ellenbogen and Jill Scipione in two gallery rooms showing paintings from her Psalms and Prophets series; these works are included in her new book of the same title, a Victory Hall Press publication, which will first be available at the Artist Reception.

Since the beginning of time, art has been made for sacred and devotional purposes by all cultures. The Divine, one's belief in a God, has been expressed in Native American and African tribal art; in the East, with works from the Hindu, Buddhist, Jewish and Islamic traditions, and in the West, in medieval Christian art through the Renaissance and into current times. Biblical Art, visual art derived from stories in the Old or New Testaments, is a significant part of the early history of art in the West.

An interest in spirituality emerged as a major concept in Modernist art at the start of the 20th century. The early abstract painter, Wassily Kandinsky wrote a 1912 treatise called "Concerning the Spiritual in Art"; and his conviction that art should be an expression of the spiritual in mankind was shared by many of his contemporaries including Mondrian, Arp, Duchamp and Malevich. For Newman, Pollock, Rothko and other American abstract expressionists of the mid-nineteen hundreds, art was primarily about spirituality. Some pursued their own spiritual quest in which many of their works were inspired by Eastern sources. Or, like Kandinsky, they saw the artist as a kind of prophet or leader of humankind's spiritual development.

In 1775, writer Edmund Burke defined the Sublime in descriptive terms of darkness, obscurity, privation, vastness, magnificence, loudness and suddenness. The Sublime, in reference to the awesomeness of nature, or of God-in-nature, was a significant conviction of artists in the Romantic period of the 18th and 19th centuries. In England, William Turner's atmospheric, turbulent sea paintings exemplified these concepts, as did the vast, majestic landscapes of early American painters such as Albert Bierstadt, Thomas Cole and Frederic Church, and in a quieter way, the German painter, Caspar David Friedrich, whose work concerned the contemplation of nature, and sought to convey the spiritual experiences of life.

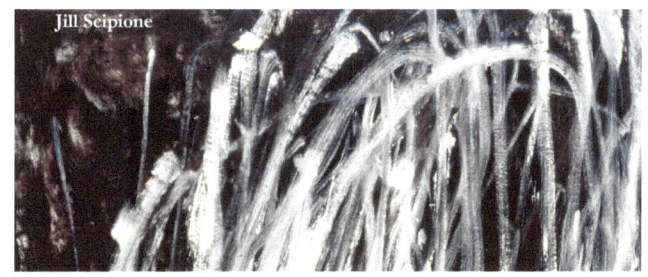

Jill Scipione

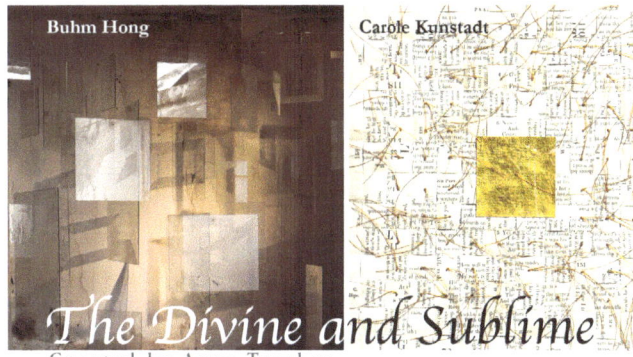

Buhm Hong   Carole Kunstadt

The Divine and Sublime
Curated by Anne Trauben

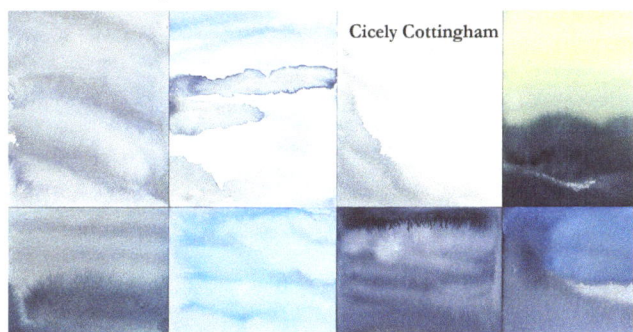

Cicely Cottingham

Victory Hall ——————————————
DRAWING ROOMS
180 GRAND ST, JERSEY CITY

Thursday -Friday 4:00pm to 7:00pm / Saturday -Sunday 2:00pm to 6:00pm

—————————————— drawingrooms.org

The Divine and Sublime
October 23 to November 22, 2015
-Reception: Sunday, October 25th (3:00pm - 6:00pm)

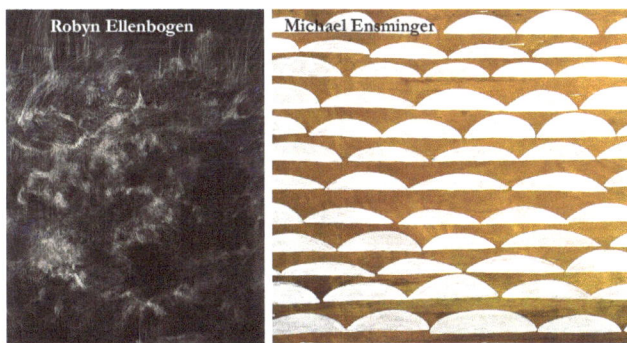

Robyn Ellenbogen   Michael Ensminger

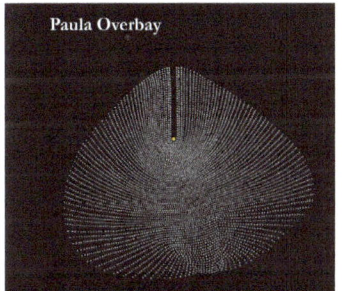

Paula Overbay

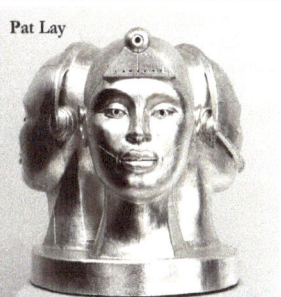

Pat Lay

This program is made possible in part by funds from the New Jersey State Council on the Arts/Department of State, a partner agency of the National Endowment for the Arts, administered by the Hudson County Office of Cultural and Heritage Affairs, Thomas A. DeGise, County Executive, and the Board of Chosen Freeholders.

VICTORY HALL PRESS

Presents albums of images by current artists in the NJ/NY area working in drawing, photography and painting. We have been publishing books since 2010 that are available on Amazon and at many other on-line booksellers as well as from area bookstores. This year, we launched our Mostly Drawing Journal, which will periodically present new works from area artists with a focus on innovative drawing.

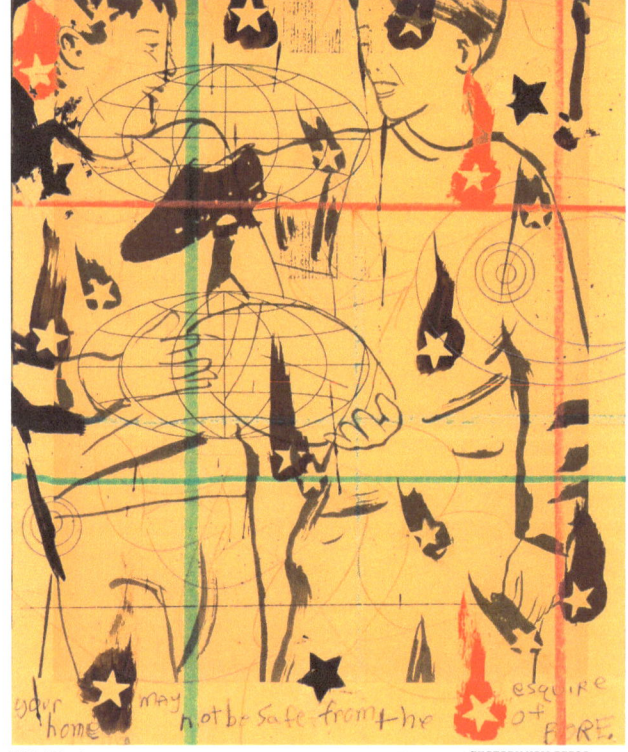

MOSTLY DRAWING a journal of current drawing

VOL. 1 No. 1   /VICTORY HALL PRESS

MOSTLY DRAWING: A JOURNAL OF CURRENT DRAWING

This gathering of works by artists involved in the Jersey City area offers twenty-five approaches to drawing and drawing-related paintings, photographic images and three-dimensional drawing. Drawing, like writing, is an essentialy human form of expression, investigation and communication. Our intention when starting Drawing Rooms as an arts center in 2012, was to promote, encourage and display developments in drawing and drawing-related works by artists in our area. In creating this journal, we want to extend our reach beyond the walls of our building and present an ever-progressing selection of artists and images to a broader public. The dea of turning these artworks into print, making something you can hold in your hand is much in keeping with these goals.

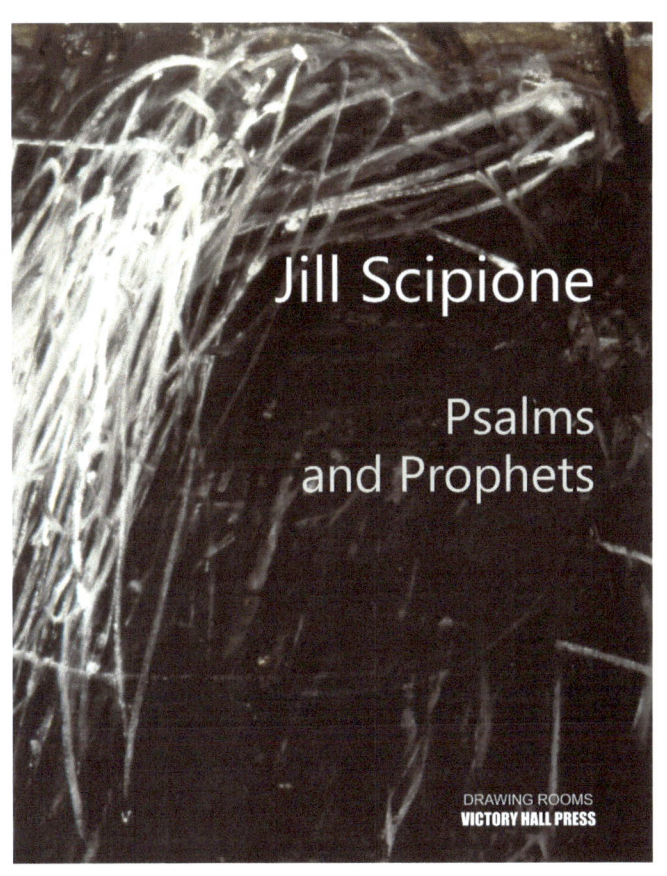

Jill Scipione: PSALMS AND PROPHETS

Authored by Victory Hall Press, Edited by James Pustorino Jill Scipione's work is about the human condition; the situation of the soul and flesh described using the physicality of drawing and painting space. The paintings gathered under the title Psalms and Prophets have direct connections to specific phrases and passages in the Biblical texts, yet also in each the artist uses these texts as inspiration for the building of a system or specific form in paint that would have its own meaning and object-quality. Each painting then becomes a physical model that embodies or serves as a companion to the textual concept.

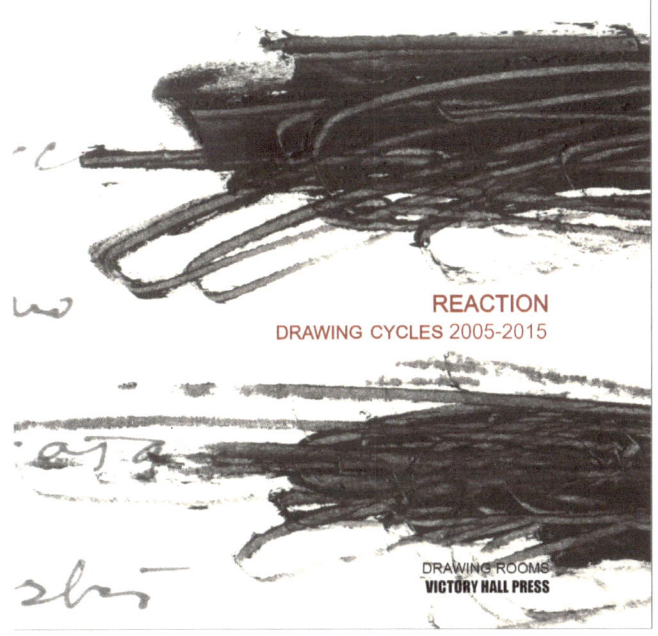

Maria Pavlovska: REACTION
Drawing Cycles 2005 - 2015
by Victory Hall Press James Pustorino, Editor

Maria Pavlovska's drawings engage this language, exploring the full range of her internal life even as her line and brush-stroke explore from the sensitive to the explosive, from freedom to order. These cycles of small drawings are notes to herself, put down on paper over a span of ten years. They have an intimate power; she will often term them 'diaries'. Specific without depiction, they are images that can be read and appreciated over time, something a person wants to keep close and refer to again and again. Just as sonnets or song cycles create strings of poetic imagery, each drawing here adds to the next like a bead on a chain, or a part of a story, a page of a book.

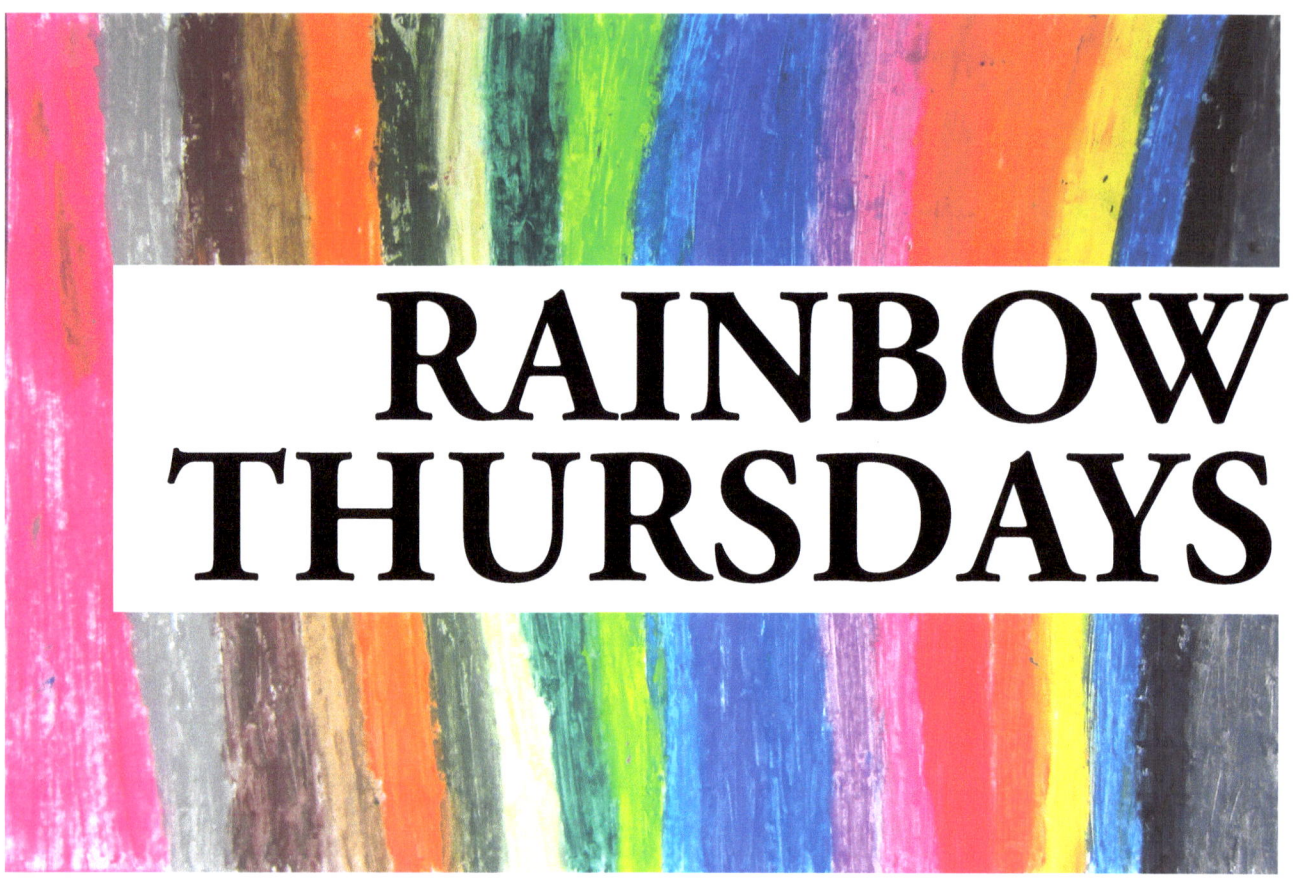

RAINBOW THURSDAYS

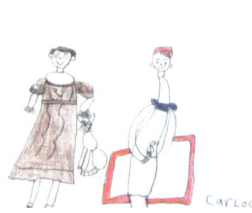 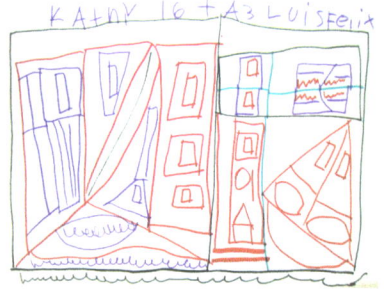 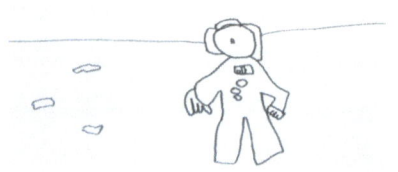

RAINBOW THURSDAYS Artists at Windmill Center is a community-based art education program that connects developmentally disabled adults with professional artists who provide them with materials and training to express themselves through art. High school students interested in art also visit as assistants.

These classes are presented free of charge.

Classes: 40 developmentally disabled adults meet weekly to learn painting and drawing with 4 teachers at Windmill Center, 5th and Broadway, Bayonne, NJ.

Up to twenty visiting artists from the NJ/NY area will also meet with the students and share their artwork and instruction.

Artists from Victory Hall Inc.'s program with developmentally disabled adults at Windmill Center, Bayonne, NJ.

Program Directors: Jill Scipione and Jim Pustorino
Teachers: Bruno Nadalin, Joyce Zielaznicki, Catherine Perry, Kathy Scipione, Ibou N'Doye.

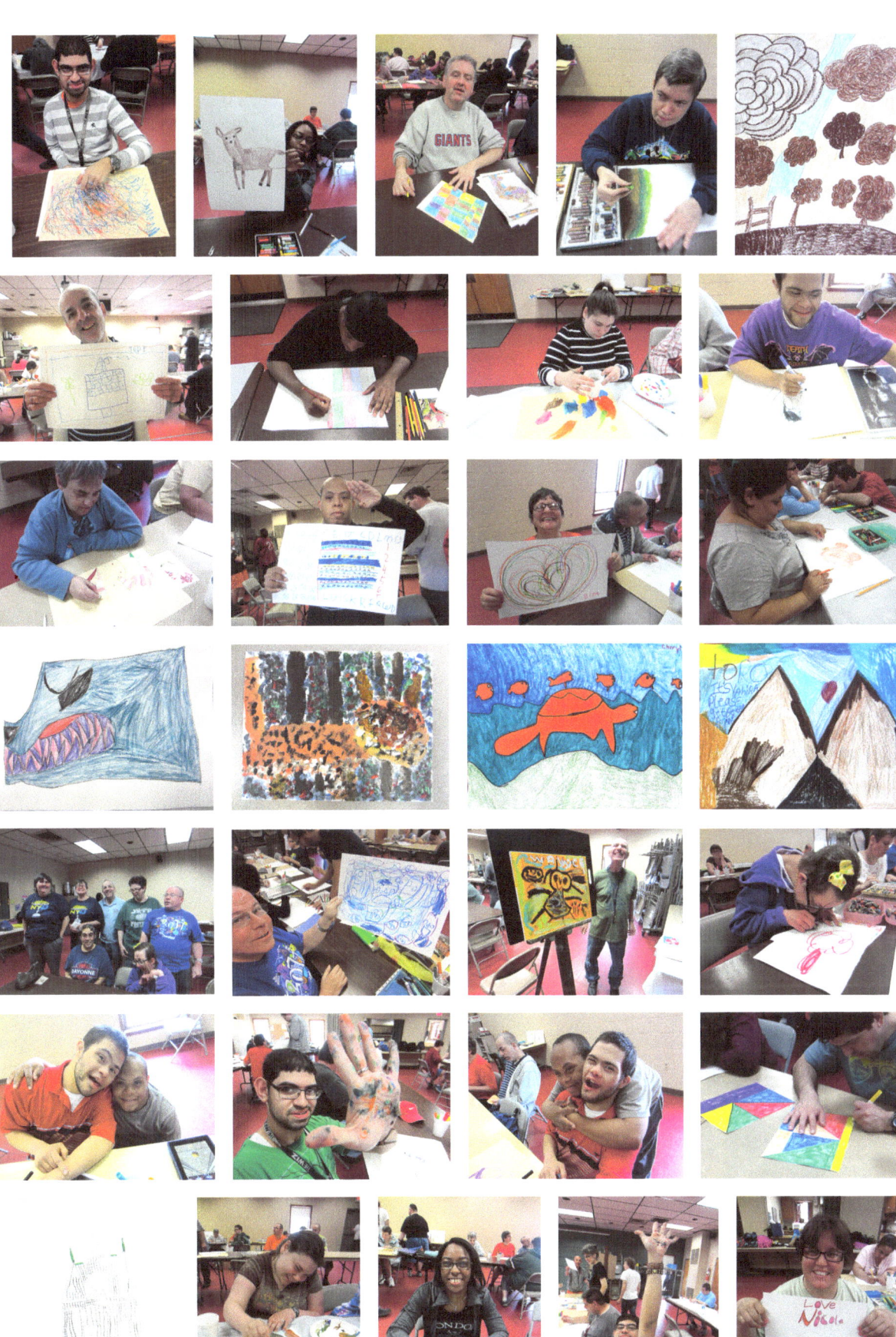

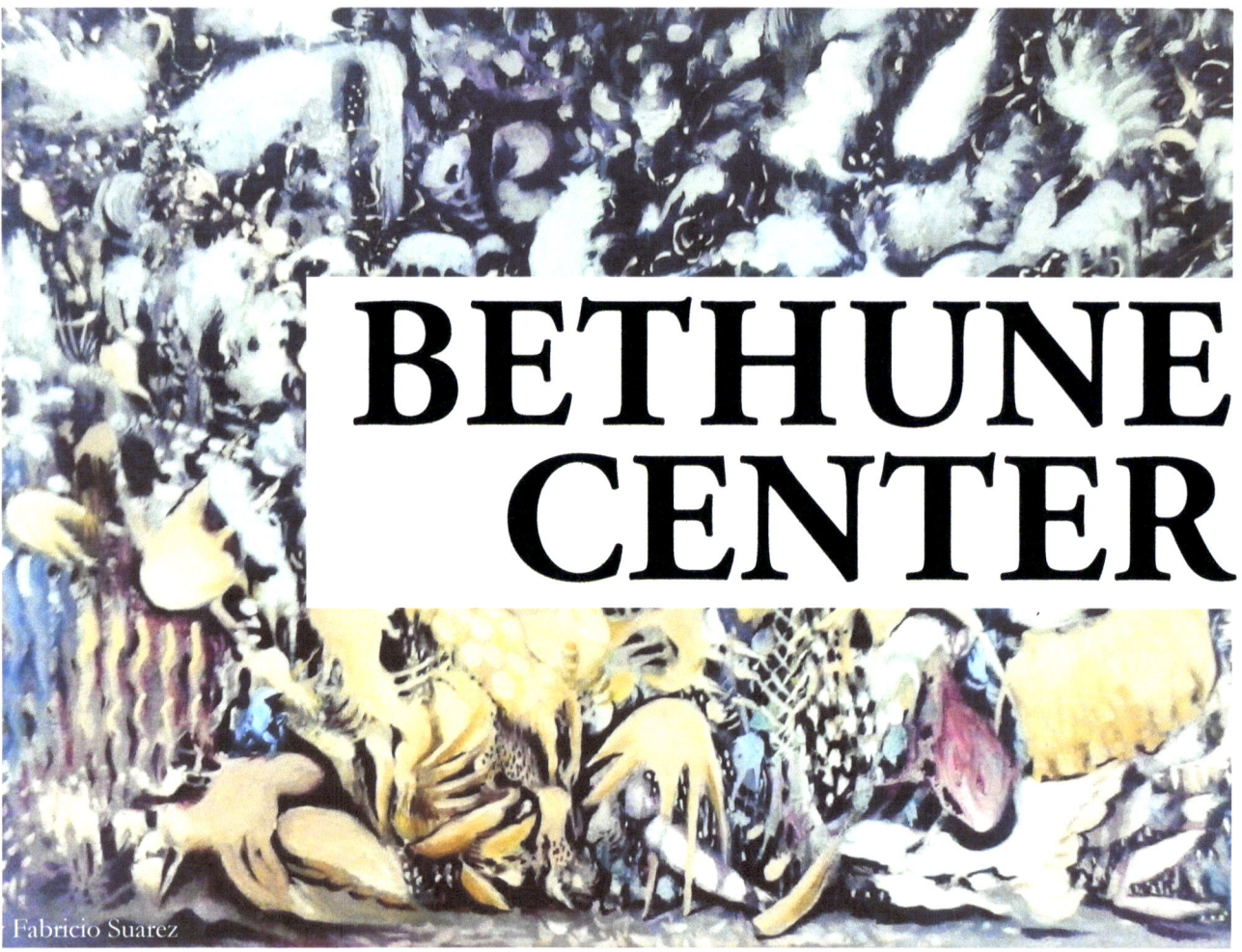

BETHUNE CENTER

Fabricio Suarez

Victory Hall is working with Director Alvin Pettit of the Mary McLeod Bethune LIFE Center in Jersey City to produce year-round exhibitions at the Bethune Center in the Greenville neighborhood of Jersey City. Curator Joyce Zielaznicki organized 4 exhibitions for the 2014 through 2015 season at the Bethune.

2015 Hispanic Heritage Art Exhibition at the Melissa Holloway Fine Art Galleries located at the Mary McLeod Bethune LIFE Center in Jersey City (September 11 through November 20, 2015).

This exhibition will celebrate artists of Hispanic heritage working in the Jersey City area, as well as an artist from India. The second part of our series of exhibitions that pay tribute to the various diverse cultures and ethnicities that make up Jersey City.

Artists: Antonio Nogueira, Leandro Comrie Pepin, Walter Rodriguez, Mauro (Fabricio) Suarez, and Jeankarlos Cruz.

Philippine and Asian Art Exhibition / Reception: Friday, June 12, 2015 (6:30pm - 9:00pm).

In celebration of Philippine Independence Day, our exhibition focuses on photography, calligraphy, painting and installation. The recent art history of the Filipino and Asian artists was influenced by international and regional biennial and triennial exhibitions held in the 1990s. These were funded by ambitious city governments eager to promote themselves as cultural hubs. At that time, museums were devoted to contemporary Asian art linked to biennales, and the curators were uniting the work of contemporary artists from diverse countries, expanding cultural communications between diverse artists. This art exhibition is on view through August 15, 2015.

Artists: Maria Araceli Francisco (Textile Artist and Educator), Gloria Pacis (Painting), Martha Garcia (Painting), Feng Xiao Liu (Photography and Calligraphy), and Tuan Minh Tran (Sculptor and Painter).

Black History Month Art Exhibition / Reception: Friday, February 13, 2015 (6:00pm -9:00pm).

The value and authentic beauty of African-American inspiration is on display at The Mary McLeod Bethune Life Center in the Jackson Hill District of Jersey City, New Jersey, from February 13 through March 20, 2015. The art exhibition expresses the ancestry of African-Americans through art as a vital contribution to the art of the United States and our community.

Throughout the Harlem Renaissance movement that spanned the 1920's people were coming to a greater appreciation of African-American art in America. While historians' Carter G. Woodson and the Rev. Jesse E. Moorland founded the Association for the Study of Negro Life and History, the organization's goal was to identify and promote the accomplishments of Americans of African descent. Coinciding with the birthdays of Abraham Lincoln and Fredrick Douglass, the community involvement across the country organized events to promote the achievements of African-Americans.

By the 1960's, a monthly celebration had developed. With the added influence of the civil rights movement – several college campuses, schools and communities in the United States proclaimed February, as Black History Month. In February, 1976, Black History Month had become official.

Artists: Mel Holston, Geraldine Anderson Gaines, and Thomas (Taiwo) Du Vall. "African Children of Zambia "Banana Leaf Four-Panel Artwork"

"Earth and Sky" December 5th – January 30th
Focuses on the world we live in, such as landscape images, the configuration of the clouds in the sky. Evoking the emotion of the scene through brush strokes, color glazes, lines and a rich palette suggested by the surroundings, the artists capture a fleeting moment, like the sun changing the landscape each second as it sets, offering a timeless remembrance of their memory. Here, various artistic conceptions of landscape—some grandiose, some intimate—are shown.

"The Human Presence in Nature"
Indicates the artist's emotional, spiritual and social composition, belief system, and adjustments to conditions in their life . As nature evolves, such just as a forest goes through an ecological succession, so do we as individuals evolve and are at present a compilation of bits and pieces of the experiences we have traveled.

Artists: Robyn Ellengbogen, Geraldine Gaines, Ibou N'Doye, Mel Holston, Gloria C. Pacis, Marilyn Scheyer-Terry, Loura Van Der Meule, Margaret Webber.

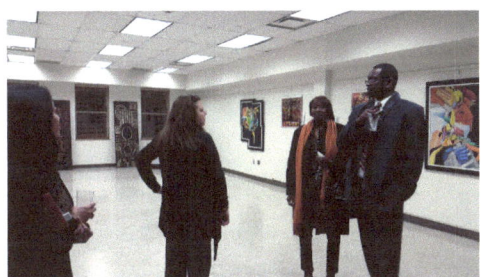
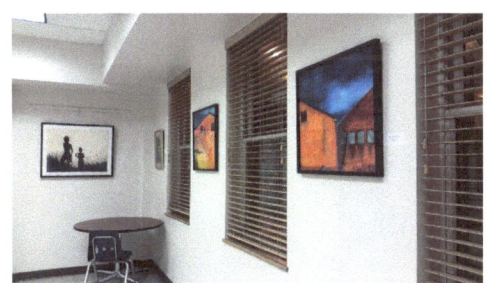
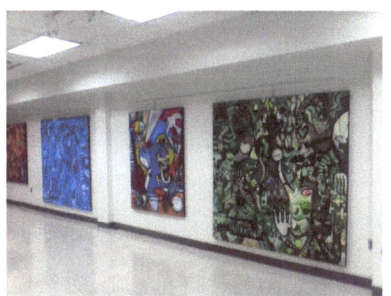
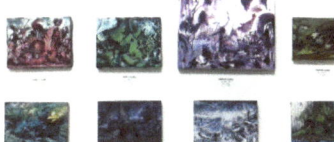
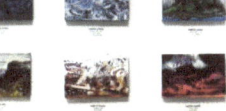
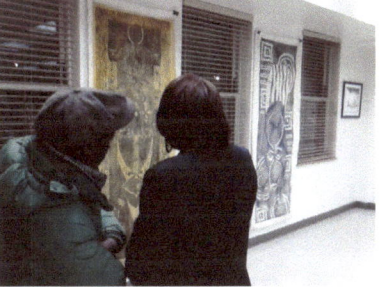
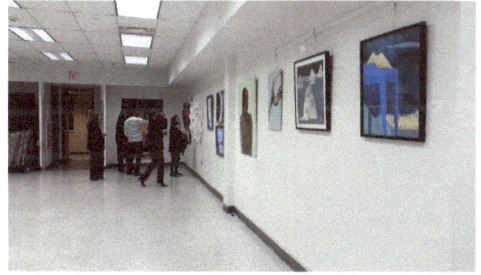

THE ART PROJECT

Victory Hall Inc. Director, James Pustorino, is collaborating with Shuster Management on THE ART PROJECT in Jersey City to develop exhibition spaces in two of their downtown buildings at 148 First St. and 109 Columbus Ave. The project exhibits area artists and promotes sales of their work to neighborhood residents. All proceeds go to the artists and a significant percentage benefits Jersey City's Bethune Center's art classes for under-served teenagers. Two year-round exhibition spaces at the Art House building at 148 First St. JC and 109 Columbus feature up to 40 artists annually in six-month-long exhibitions. A separate catalogue is produced featuring all the artists for each exhibition.

Artists for the 2015 season include:

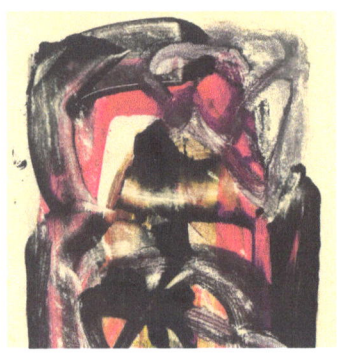
Agnes de Bethune

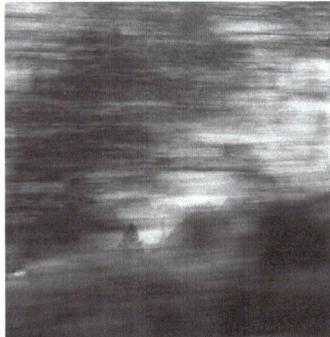
Edward Fausty

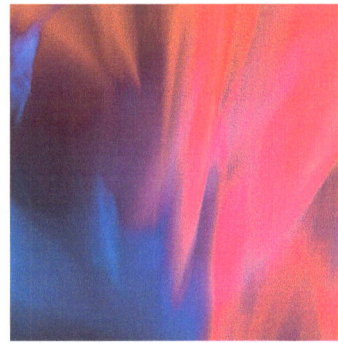
Geoffrey Sokol

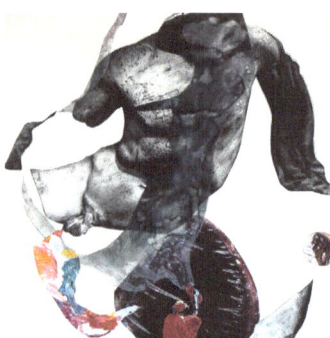
Jane R. Dell

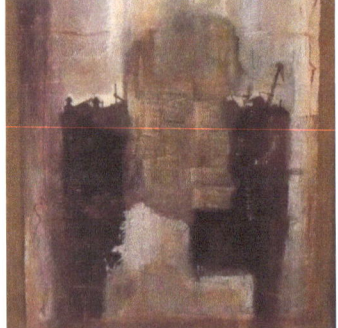
Cheryl Gross

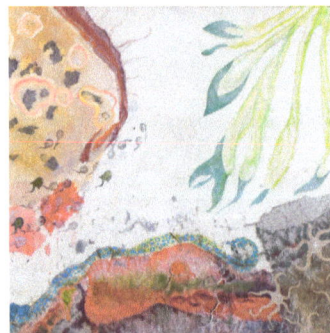
Eileen Ferara

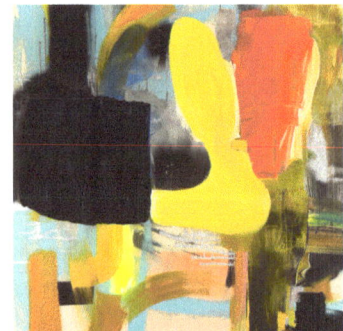
Glenn Garver

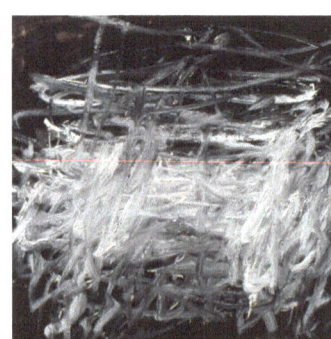
Jill Scipione

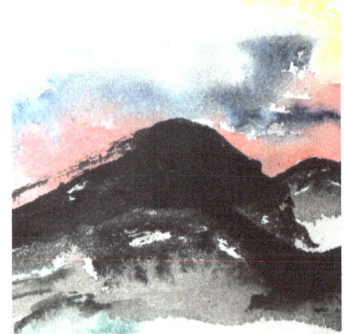
Deirdre Kennedy

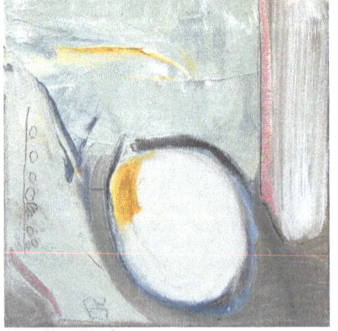
Gail Winbury

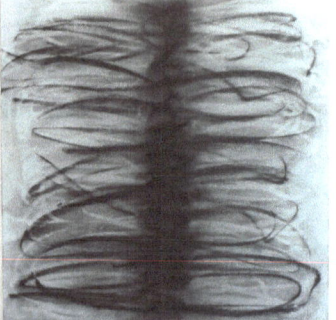
Heidi Curko

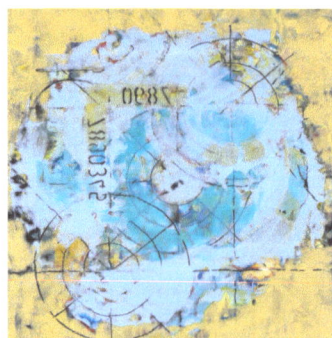
Kathy Cantwell

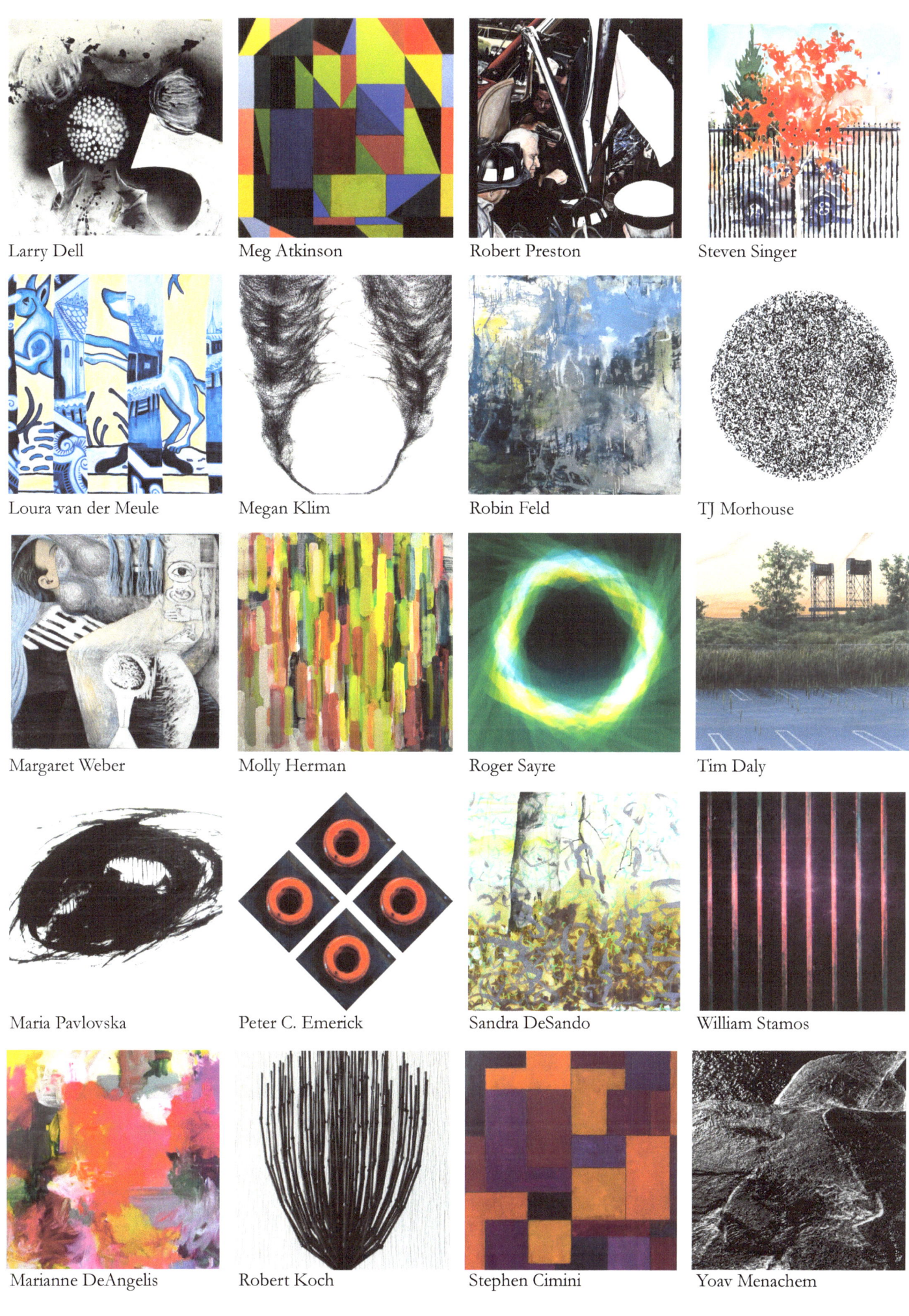

Larry Dell

Meg Atkinson

Robert Preston

Steven Singer

Loura van der Meule

Megan Klim

Robin Feld

TJ Morhouse

Margaret Weber

Molly Herman

Roger Sayre

Tim Daly

Maria Pavlovska

Peter C. Emerick

Sandra DeSando

William Stamos

Marianne DeAngelis

Robert Koch

Stephen Cimini

Yoav Menachem

HAND -IN- HAND
ART SCHOOL

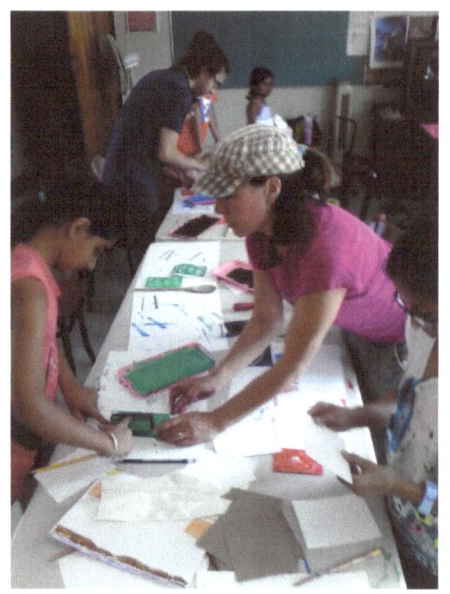

This year, Victory Hall Inc. collaborated with Hand-in-Hand Music School in Bayonne, to launch Hand-in-Hand Art School. The Hand-in-Hand program encourages young people to consider themselves artists, both musical and visual, and to see creativity as an important part of their life.

The Hand-in-Hand afterschool program at Grace Lutheran Church Avenue C and 37th St., Bayonne focuses on drawing, painting, collage and sculpture as a basis for exploration of our interior and exterior worlds. The program puts students in touch with professional artists who share their knowledge and work alongside the students. Visiting artists regularly introduce new concepts through one-day workshops both at class time and in our Workshop Festival Days.

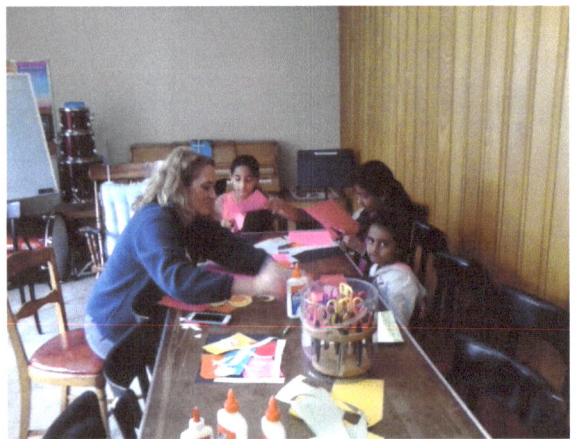

Artists:

Kimberley Wiseman

Jill Scipione

Bruno Nadalin

Eileen Ferara

Ibou Ndoye

Anne Trauben

Maggie Ens

Hand in Hand Director: Pastor Gary Grindeland
Art School Director: James Pustorino

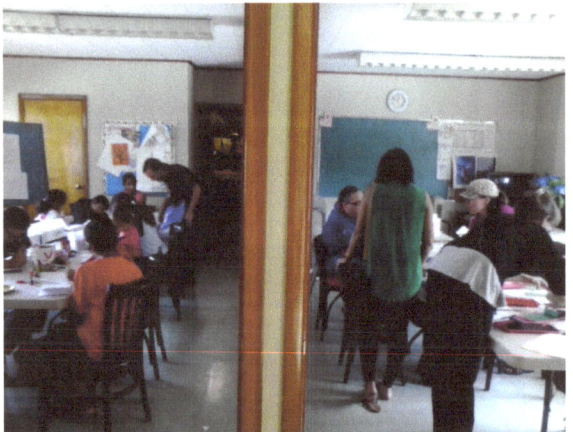

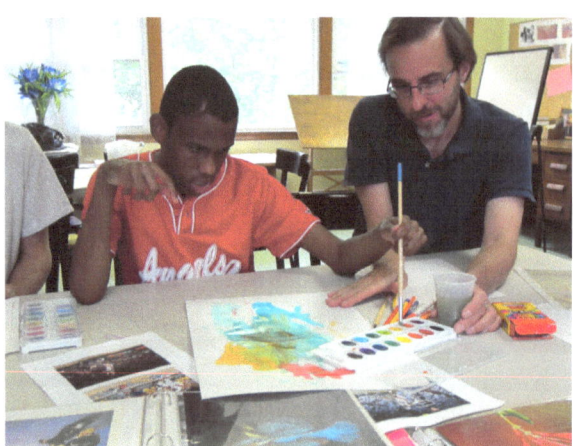

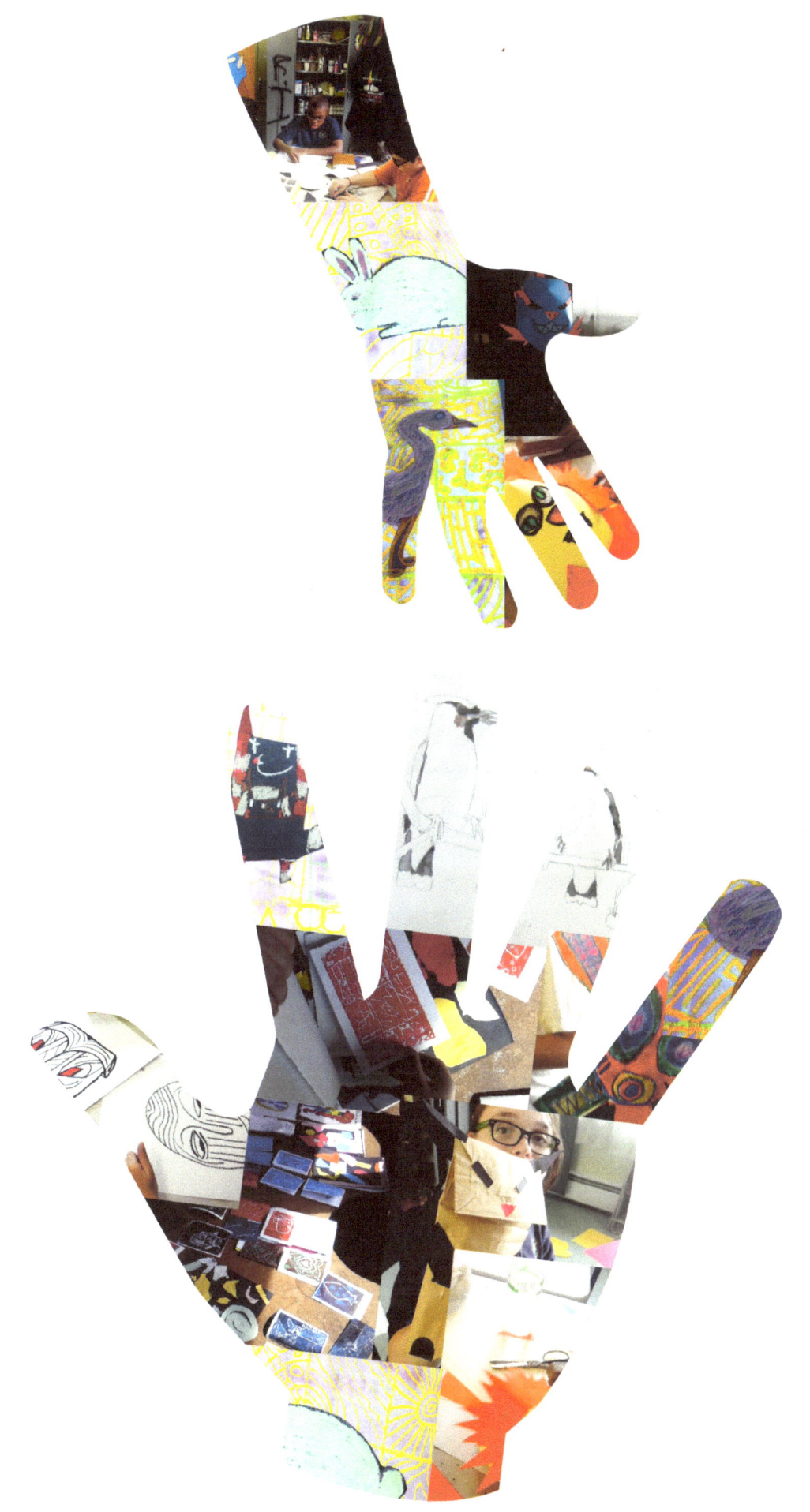

ARTIST WORKSPACES
3RD FLOOR AT DRAWING ROOMS

The Artist's' WorkSpace Program at Drawing Rooms has been developing on the third floor of our art center building at 180 Grand St.

Renovating the third floor of our former convent building and creating spaces for both individual artist studios and shared work areas and classrooms has been moving forward this year.

Artists who form the core of our organization are able to rent studios and will be sharing their work with the public during Open Studio weekends throughout the year.

Class and work areas for children and adults are starting this January, including Public School workshops in collaboration with Jersey City Board of Education and evening programs that introduce adults to the concepts of art-making.

A great addition to our second floor exhibition rooms, the WorkSpaces create a place where artists can work together and invite the public into the art-making process.

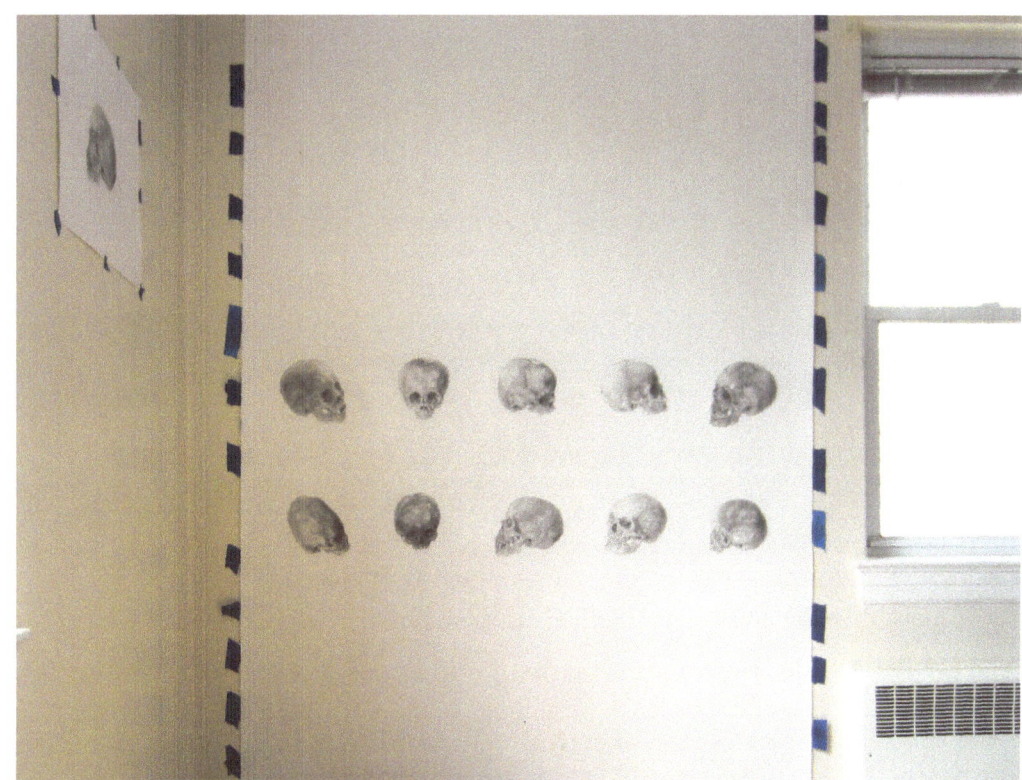

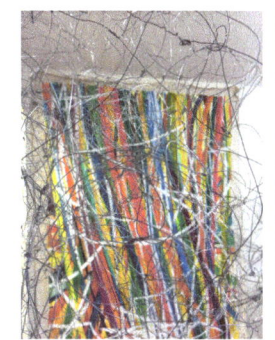
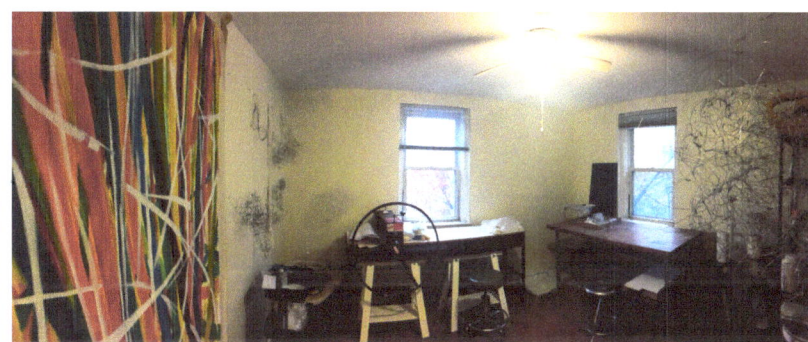
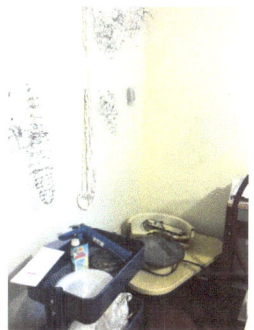

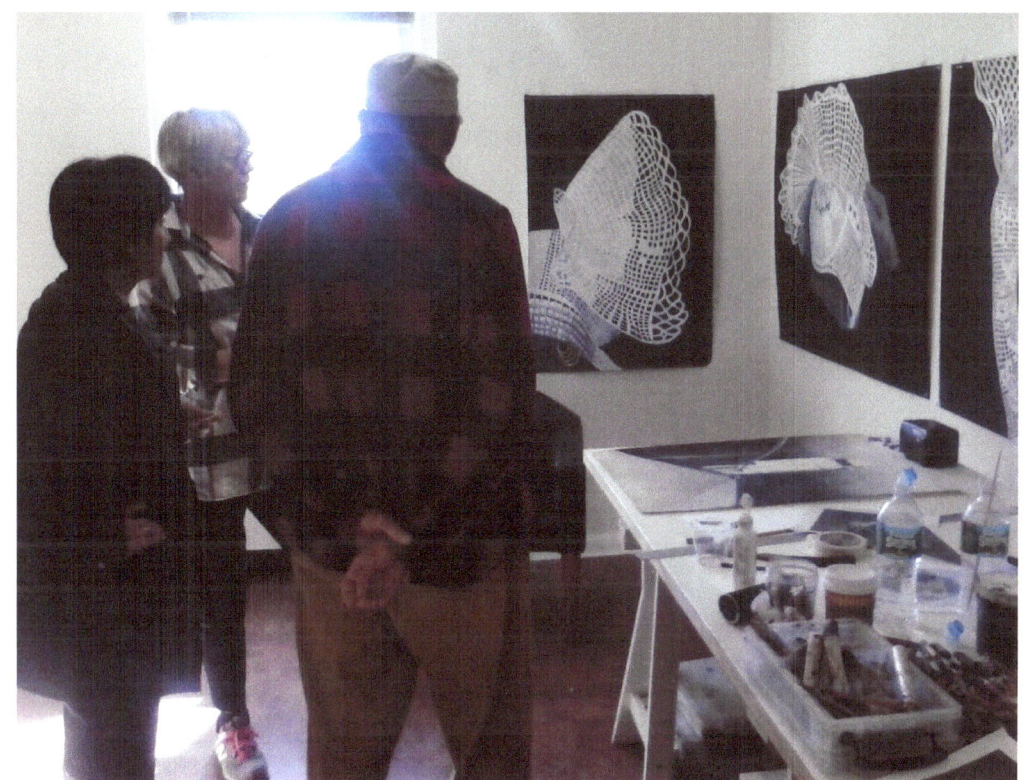

THANKS TO OUR DONORS FOR THE BIG SMALL SHOW

Komegashi Japanese Restaurant
The Light Horse Tavern
Edward's Steak House

Thanks to all the Artists who donated their work to The Big Small Show Fundraiser Auction:

Alan Walker	Dora Tomulic	Kerry Kolenut	Roger Sayre
Alyce Gottesman	Duda Penteado	Leslie Kerby	Stephen Cimini
Beth Dary	Ed Fausty	Lisa Ficarelli-Halpern	Steve Singer
Bill Stamos	Eileen Ferara	Margaret Neill	Susan Evans Grove
Binnie Birstein	Ellen Hackl Fagan	Maria Pavlovska	Tamar Zinn
Bruce Halpin	Etty Yaniv	Marianne DeAngelis	Theresa DeSalvio
Carol Radsprecher	Feng Xiao Liu	Marsha Goldberg	Tim Daly
Carole Kunstadt	Gail Winbury	Meg Atkinson	Tomomi Ono
Catherine Haggerty	Giovanna Cecchetti	Michael Ensminger	Trix Rosen
Charles Kessler	Jane Dell	Mona Brody	Valerie Huhn
Claire McConaughy	Jaynie Crimmins	Muriel Favaro	Winifred McNeill
Dasha Bazanova	Jeanne Brasile	Pat Lay	and others
Diane Englander	Jennifer Krause Chapeau	Paula Overbay	
Diane Tenerelli-June	Jodie Fink	Robin Feld	
Deirdre Kennedy	Kay Kenny	Robyn Ellenbogen	

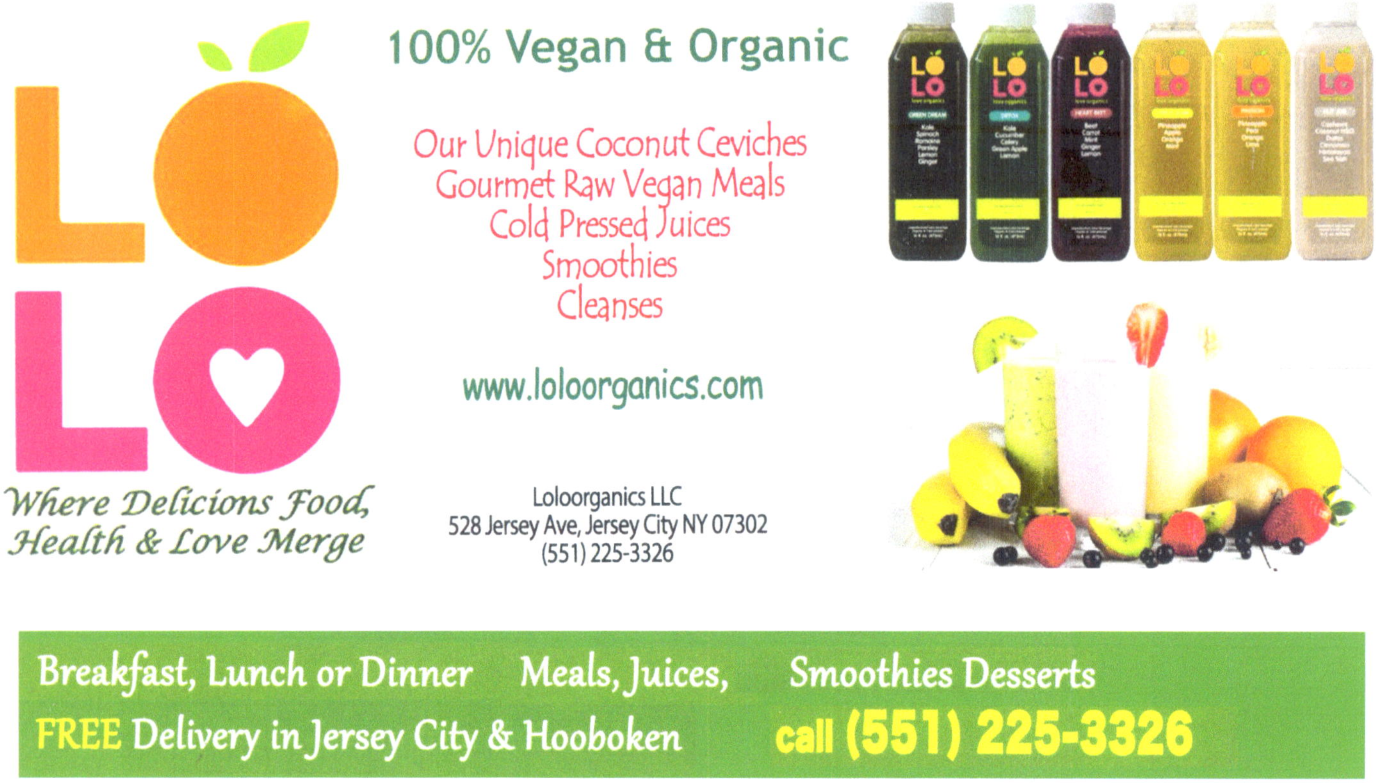

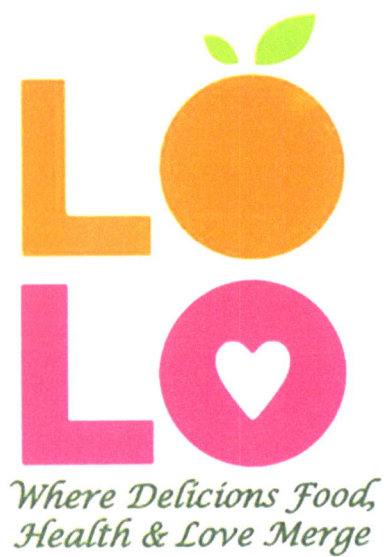
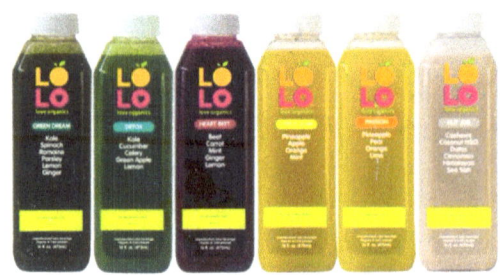
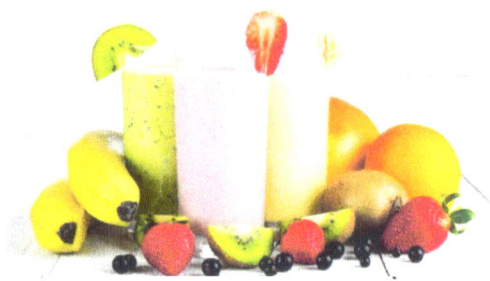

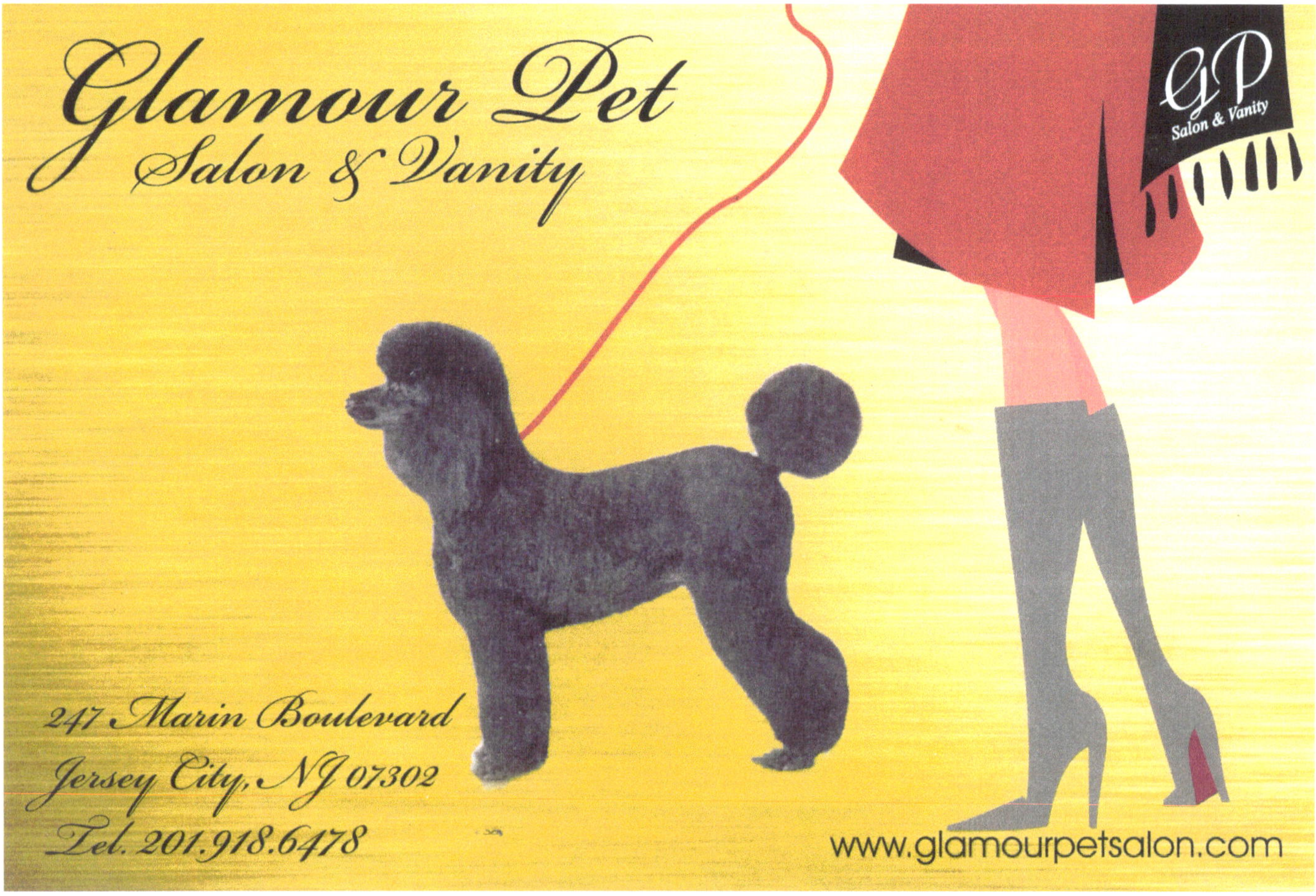

2016 EXHIBITIONS

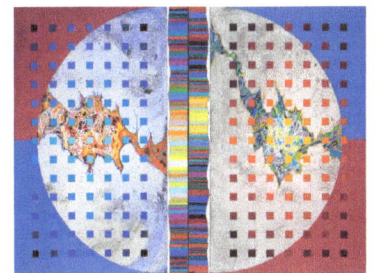

Gian Berto Vanni
through January 29, 2016

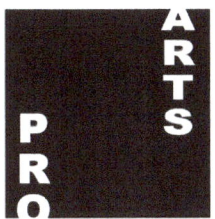

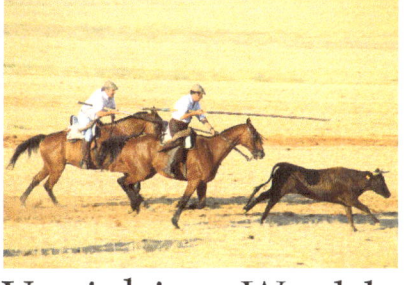

Vanishing Worlds
February 1 - April 15, 2016

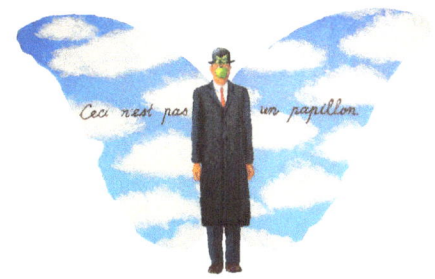

Under the Influence
Fall 2016

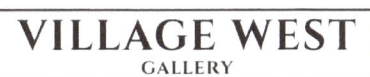

VILLAGE WEST
GALLERY

331 NEWARK AVE | JERSEY CITY, NJ 07302
VILLAGEWESTGALLERY.COM

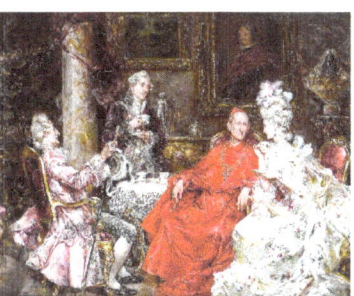

Ancien Régime
Winter 2016-17

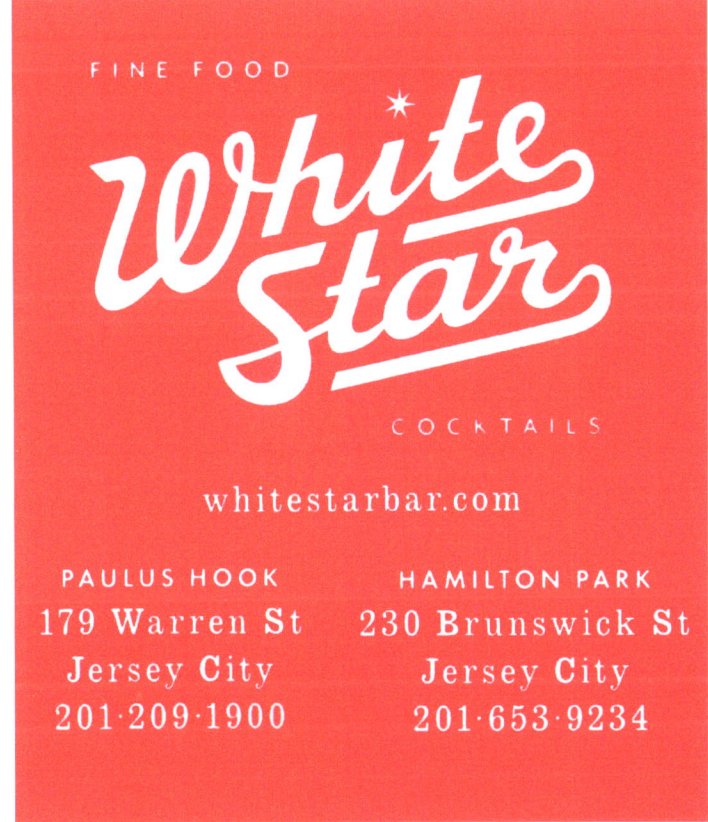
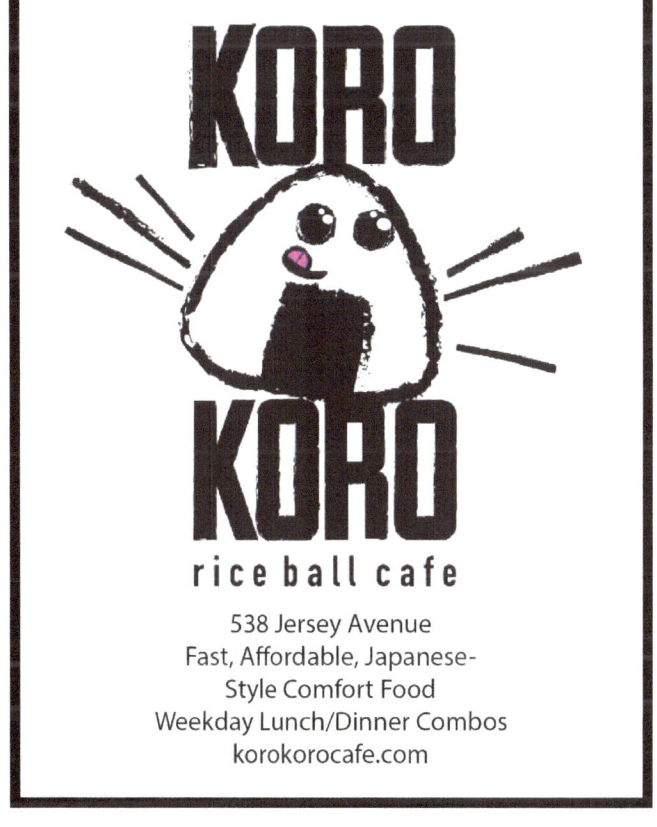

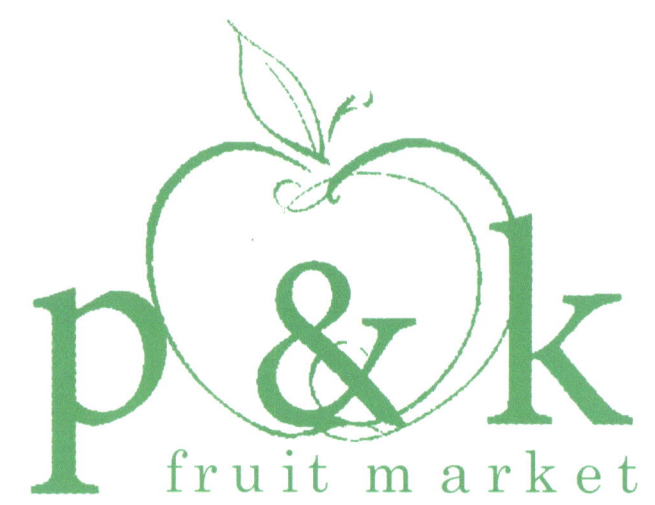

p & k

fruit market

170 Newark Avenue, Jersey City, NJ 07302

8am - 9pm daily

(201) 451-9888

info@pkfruitmarket.com

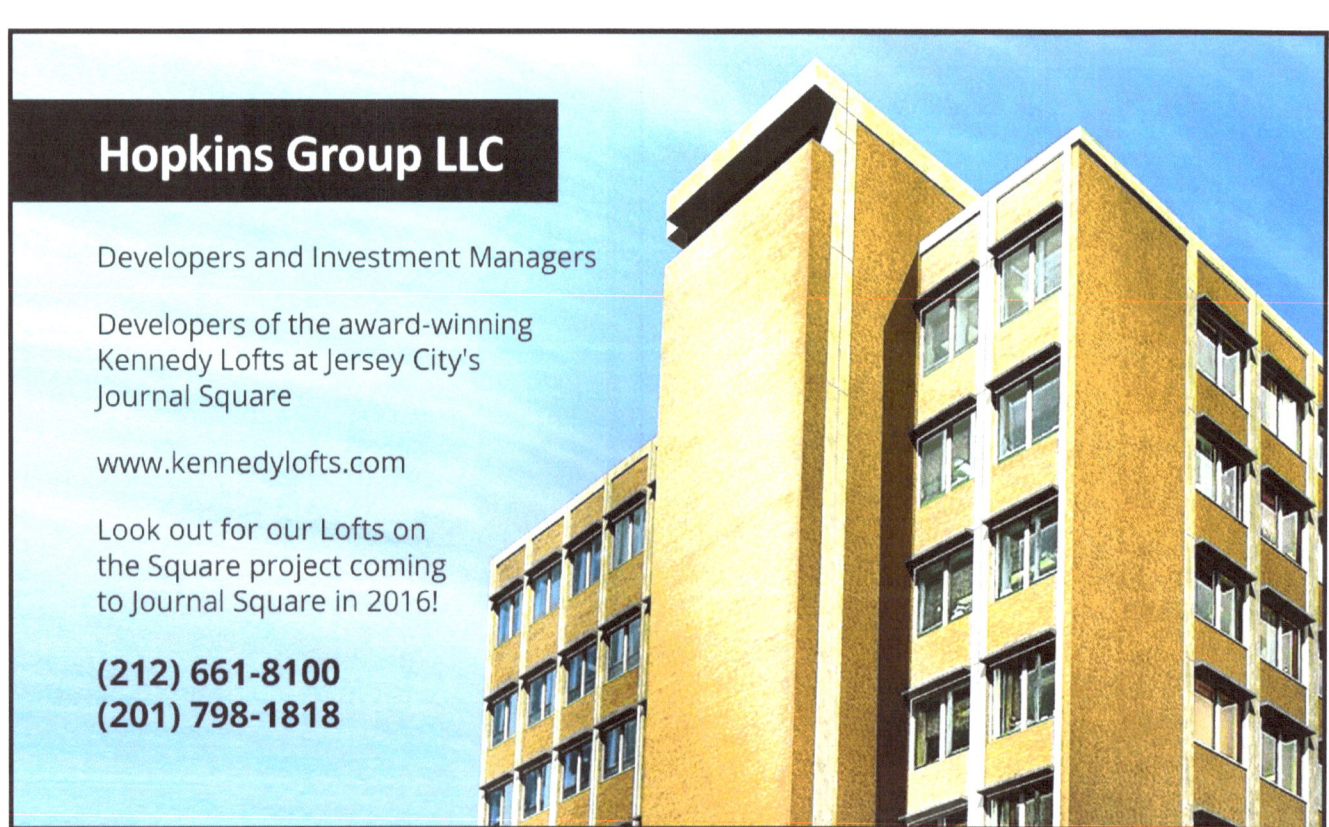

"At Swim Stars our mission is to provide quality swim lessons to all of our Swim Star clients"

870 Montgomery Street
Jersey City, NJ 07306
http://www.swimstars.biz/

Swim Stars

S W I M   S C H O O L

Thanks to all our 2015 sponsors!

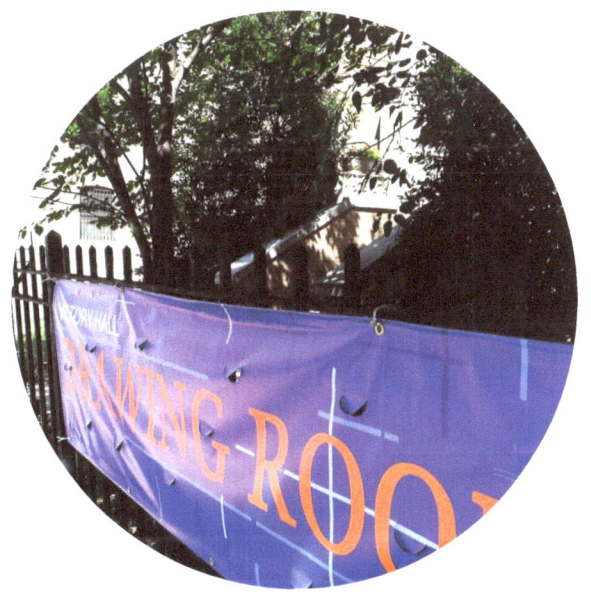

To sponsor an AD HERE,
email: danielle@drawingrooms.org

www.ingramcontent.com/pod-product-compliance
Lightning Source LLC
Chambersburg PA
CBHW050902180526
45159CB00007B/2763